THOUGHTS:
AN ESSAY ON CONTENT

Aristotelian Society Series

Volume 1
COLIN MCGINN
Wittgenstein on Meaning:
An Interpretation and Evaluation

Volume 2
BARRY TAYLOR
Modes of Occurrence:
Verbs, Adverbs and Events

Volume 3
KIT FINE
Reasoning With Arbitrary Objects

Aristotelian Society Monographs Committee:
Anthony Savile (Monographs Editor)
Martin Davies
Jennifer Hornsby

*This volume edited for the Aristotelian Society
by Martin Davies.*

Christopher Peacocke

Thoughts:
An Essay on Content

Aristotelian Society Series

Volume 4

Basil Blackwell · Oxford

First published 1986
in cooperation with The Aristotelian Society
King's College, London WC2R 2LS

Basil Blackwell Publisher Ltd
108 Cowley Road, Oxford OX4 1JF, England

Basil Blackwell Inc.
432 Park Avenue South, Suite 1505
New York, NY 10016, USA

British Library Cataloguing in Publication Data

Peacocke, Christopher
Thoughts : an essay on content.
1. Thought and thinking
I. Title
153.4'2   BF455

ISBN 0–631–14674–1

Library of Congress Cataloging Publication Data

Peacocke, Christopher.
Thoughts: an essay on content.
1. Thought and thinking—Addresses, essays, lectures.
2. Knowledge, Theory of—Addresses, essays, lectures.
I. Title.
B105.T54P42 1985   121   85–20050
ISBN 0–631–14674–1

Photoset and printed in Great Britain by
Photobooks (Bristol) Ltd

Contents

To my parents

Preface

I started the first continuous draft of this material when I was a Fellow of the Center for Advanced Study in the Behavioral Sciences at Stanford in the academic year 1983-4; that first draft was completed when I was a Visiting Research Associate of the Center for the Study of Language and Information on the Stanford campus in the summer of 1984. Without the generous support and superb facilities of each of these institutions, it is certain that this work would not have existed. I also wish to thank Oxford University and the Governing Body of New College, Oxford, both of which granted me additional leave of absence beyond my contractual rights. I am grateful too for financial support from the National Science Foundation (grant BNS 76-22943) and the British Academy. It has naturally made a deep impression on me that the major sources of support for this work were American, support granted without one eye on the nationality of the recipient.

The material here was presented to seminars in Oxford in Michaelmas Term 1982 and Hilary Term 1985; some of it was also discussed in a joint seminar in Oxford with Donald Davidson in Michaelmas 1984. Some early drafts of the material on epistemology and content were given in three talks to the MIT Philosophy Colloquium in October 1983. I drew upon slightly earlier versions of the second and third chapters in a paper 'What Determines Truth Conditions?', to appear in *Subject, Thought and Context*, edited by John McDowell and

Philip Pettit (Oxford: Oxford University Press, 1986). The rest of the material appears here for the first time. I have been helped by the discussion of this work whenever I have presented it, and especially by the detailed comments on written versions given to me by Joseph Almog, Akeel Bilgrami, Simon Blackburn, Michael Dummett, Graeme Forbes, Richard Grandy, Jennifer Hornsby, Brian Loar, John McDowell, Stephen Schiffer and Stephen Stich. I thank Marianne Talbot for compiling the index. My greatest personal debt is to Martin Davies, whose advice – both substantive and editorial – has improved almost every page of the essay.

June 1985   Christopher Peacocke

                                         King's College
                                         London WC2R 2LS

One thing that 'makes thought thought' . . . is that thought is sound or unsound, *i.e.* thought has normative epistemic properties . . . I myself cannot believe that an account of 'what makes thought thought' which leaves us in the dark as to the nature and origin of these properties could be correct.

Hilary Putnam, 'Reflexive Reflections', *Erkenntnis* **22** (1985), pp. 143–153, at pp. 148–149.

1

The Idea of a Theory of Content

Questions of the form 'What is it to possess a given concept?' arise in almost every area of philosophy. Whether the topic is causation, or identity, or generality, or consciousness, or objectivity, such questions are central and pivotal. In the discussion of these questions, there ought to be an interaction between a general theory of concept possession and the phenomena of the particular area discussed. In one direction, manifest facts about the concepts we do exercise in a particular area must be accommodated by a general theory of concept possession. In the other direction, a proposal about grasp of a particular concept must be rejected if it is not consistent with a good general theory.

Concepts are constituents of whole contents which may be judged true or false. Facts about a concept supervene on facts about the contents in which it occurs; so a general theory of concept possession must be part of a general theory of content. This essay aims to sketch the outlines of a general, substantive theory of content. There are several terms of art in this statement of aim: let us take 'content' first.

I use 'content' and 'Thought' as stylistic variants, and take Thoughts to have the four properties Frege attributed to them.[1] Thoughts have absolute truth values, without relativization to anything else; they are composite, structured entities;

[1] G. Frege, *Logical Investigations*, tr. P. Geach (Oxford: Blackwell, 1977).

they are the objects of belief, intention, hope and the other attitudes; and it can be that one and the same Thought is judged, argued about or agreed upon by two different thinkers. We can strip away the spatial metaphors which Frege used to convey his doctrine of Thoughts: the core that remains is the thesis that there are contents which have all four of these properties.

On this conception, the Thought George expresses when he says 'I'm cold' must be a much richer thing than the neo-Russellian proposition represented by the triple consisting of George himself, the property of being cold, and the time of the utterance. That proposition would equally correspond to an utterance of 'George is cold': and we know that an amnesiac, for instance, could believe the Thought expressed in the first utterance without believing the Thought expressed in the second. For many purposes, as has also become familiar, important distinctions can be drawn not at the level of particular Thoughts, but at the level of what I will call types of Thought. When George thinks to himself 'I'm cold' and you think to yourself 'I'm cold', you think Thoughts of the same type. Two people also think Thoughts of the same type if they are presented in visual perception with qualitatively identical cars, from the same relative point of view, and both, on such a basis, judge something of the form 'That car is blue'. One could give a definition of sameness of type of Thought in each of the current theories of indexicals: but that would be too restrictive. We also need a notion of sameness of type for recognitionally-based ways of thinking of objects, and for properties too. I will use this notion of type intuitively for now.

That there can be anything possessing all four Fregean properties is a controversial claim. But the claim that there can be any such thing is not essential to what I shall be arguing, and I will use the Fregean framework partly for ease of formulation.[2]

---

[2] Though I shall be quantifying over modes of presentation, it should not be assumed that the account I offer is necessarily in competition with a theory cast in terms of states of affairs, situations or even possible worlds. A sufficient condition for the consistency of such a theory with my own is this: that one of the two is interpretable in the other in the sense of A. Tarski, A. Mostowski and R. Robinson's *Undecidable Theories* (Amsterdam: North-Holland, 1953), pp. 20–21. This sense requires that there are possible definitions of the nonlogical constants of the one theory which when conjoined with the other yield all the theorems of the first theory as theorems.

For instance, one of the questions I will be considering is the nature of the relation between normative conditions governing the acceptance of a content and its truth conditions. Even if the Fregean framework is superseded, we can still formulate the question. In any plausible theory, there will be something which is the object of propositional attitudes; and in any plausible theory, what is believed must somehow determine a truth value. So of any plausible theory, we can ask: what is the relation between the normative conditions governing belief in something and the conditions for what is believed to determine the truth value *true*?

A second term of art was used in describing the desired theory as substantive. By a substantive theory, I mean a theory which goes beyond a concern solely with either the structural constituents or the philosophical logic of contents. A substantive theory of a given form of content should answer the question 'What is it for a subject to grasp, to be capable of judging, contents of that form?'. A substantive theory of content ought to contain a general part stating the general form that an answer to such a question must take. In addition there will be parts giving answers of the favoured general form for specific types of content: these will be of particular interest when they treat philosophically problematic concepts. This twofold division corresponds to a similar division in the theory of meaning, a division between a statement of the general form of theories of meaning and theories of the meaning of particular expressions. To supply anything approaching a full substantive theory of content would be a massive task. As Strawson said of the parallel case of a theory of meaning, it is a task neither for a single occasion nor for just one person.[3] I hope to be offering some structures of scaffolding which, with some repositioning, will help in building such a theory.

I will be offering an account on which the identity of a content is determined by certain normative conditions relating to acceptance of the content. Chapter 2 states a general conjecture relating such acceptance conditions to truth conditions: positions which would confirm this general conjecture

---

[3] 'Meaning and Truth', repr. in his *Logico-Linguistic Papers* (London: Methuen, 1971).

are elaborated successively for observational contents, quantification, contents concerning the inaccessible and for negation. This linear ordering of the topics does not reflect relations of conceptual dependence. On the contrary, the ability to think about inaccessible places, for instance, is mentioned in the account of grasp of universal quantification. Like the branches which support a tepee, the accounts are held in place in part by their relations to one another.

The notion of canonical evidence, which featured prominently in my book *Sense and Content*[4], has been dropped in this work. It is replaced in some of its roles by canonical grounds, in others by canonical commitments. There was in *Sense and Content* an inchoate conception of the relations between the evidential conditions for judging a content and the content's truth conditions: the desire to think through and be more explicit about such a conception was one of the origins of the present essay. Many of the claims framed in *Sense and Content* using the idea of canonical evidence can emigrate to and survive in the territory dimly glimpsed in this work: they may be healthier for the move.

It is also a thesis of this material that we need to draw on a substantive theory of content in giving an account of what it is for someone to *know* a particular content. One of the chapters below, Chapter 9, is not on the theory of content (and may be read as a self-contained unit). It is stage-setting for the later appearance of a claim in Chapter 10 which connects the apparatus of the substantive theory of content with an account of knowledge.

The idea of the content of an individual belief or sentence has been so powerfully criticized by writers from W.V. Quine to Hartry Field that one can hardly just take the acceptability of the notion as granted. I have tried throughout to meet these criticisms, though the sceptic about content must at some points be patient. One cannot argue that a certain theory is immune to a particular criticism without first stating the theory. The theses on knowledge should also be taken as relevant to the evaluation of scepticism about the very idea of content. If an account of knowledge really does have to draw

---

[4] Oxford: Oxford University Press, 1983.

on distinctions drawn from a substantive theory of content, then scepticism about the notion of content requires scepticism about the concept of knowledge.

Some writers, not themselves sceptical about the idea of the content of an attitude, would nevertheless say the apparatus I have used even in stating the problems is to be avoided. Stalnaker, for example, writes that if the objects of belief and other attitudes are individuated by epistemic possibility, we will be precluded from giving an explanation of intentionality in non-intentional terms.[5] But here we have to be careful to respect a distinction. Fregean contents are certainly conceived of as conforming to the principle – "Frege's Principle" – that if it is possible rationally to believe that p and not to believe that q, then the contents that p and that q are distinct. However it is one thing for a domain of entities to conform to a principle, another for their individuation to be elucidated by mentioning that principle. It is open for a Fregean to hold these two theses simultaneously: (i) it is a condition of adequacy on a theory of content that the contents it recognizes conform to Frege's Principle, and (ii) that a substantive theory of content which explains what it is for a thinker to be capable of judging a given content should not appeal directly to Frege's Principle, but should rather entail it.[6] This is just the position I will be adopting. To assess whether such a Fregean can consistently allow an explanation of intentionality in nonintentional terms, one has to look not just to what objects he assigns to the propositional attitudes, but to his substantive theory of content. This may entail, exclude or be neutral on the possibility of an explanation of intentionality in nonintentional terms. I have formulated the claims of this essay so that they remain neutral on this issue: my theses are independent of the

---

[5] *Inquiry* (Cambridge, Mass.: MIT Press, 1984), pp. 24–25.

[6] There is a parallel here with the structure of part of Wiggins' theory of identity. On this theory, any relation which is genuinely identity must conform to the schema

$$\forall x \forall y \ (x = y \rightarrow (\varphi(x) \leftrightarrow \varphi(y))).$$

But for each kind of entity, there is a "substantive" account of the individuation of members of that kind, and conformity to the schema is a *consequence* of that account. See David Wiggins, *Sameness and Substance* (Oxford: Blackwell, 1980), Chapters 1 and 2.

possibility of such an explanation. To give such an explanation consistently with the claims of this essay, one would have to give nonintentional explanations of such concepts as judging something for a certain reason and of the representational content of perceptual experience. These remarks do, though, place me implicitly in agreement with Stalnaker on the following conditional: if a theorist appeals *only* to Frege's Principle in his account of content, and does not offer any substantive theory of content, then it is not clear that *he* leaves room for the possibility of a nonintentional explanation of the intentional.

What is the relation between a theory of normative acceptance conditions and the theories of the cognitive psychologist? Suppose we had, for a given state with content – say a belief that *p* for some particular *p* – a complete explanatory account of the structures and processes which could, for a given individual, lead to his being in that state, together with a similar account of the causal consequences for this subject of his being in it. Such a theory would not use normative notions, nor would it use such mixes of normative and causal notions as that of something being someone's reason for believing something. The theorist would be *right* not to use such notions. His goal was to give an explanatory theory, not a normative one: and if he were to use the notion of something being someone's reason for being in a state, he would be open to the charge of not having eliminated intentional notions in his causal explanation, and correlatively of not having offered a theory which is wholly at the subpersonal level.[7] If the phrase 'his reason for being in the state' occurred in a research paper in cognitive psychology, we would expect the author to insist that this is a *façon de parler* that could be translated out.

This is not to imply that a normative characterization of contents will be consistent with just any old cognitive psychology of a subject whose mental states have those contents. At a minimum, there may be supervenience of the contents, normatively individuated, of a subject's states upon

---

[7] See Daniel Dennett's essays in *Brainstorms* (Montgomery, Vt.: Bradford Books, 1978).

the characterizations given by an empirical psychology of that subject which employs descriptions relating him to his environment. But the crucial point for present purposes is that an empirical theory of cognitive psychology does not *state* what the normative properties of contents are: it has different, equally important, goals. That it does not state these properties is a point which can be maintained even if some very strong reduction of intentional states to nonintentional states can be given. My aim in making these remarks is not in any way to downgrade the philosophical issues raised by cognitive psychology, which are surely genuine, difficult and fundamental. My aim is merely to delineate the level at which I shall be operating in this essay.

Even on the level at which I am operating, my discussion leaves untouched many topics which are inextricably involved with my chosen subjects. I am particularly conscious of this in relation to the limits of the intelligibility of radical scepticism, the nature of rule-following, the justification of deduction, and the nature of the content of experience. It is an entirely open possibility that work on these topics may undermine various features of my position in this essay. I hope that others, besides improving or correcting the claims for which I do argue, will consider further the relation of these topics to a substantive theory of content.

Finally, the reader will soon discover that there are far more references here to the writings of Michael Dummett than to those of anyone else, and that most of these references are in disagreement with him. It is not just the depth and originality of Dummett's views that prompts so much discussion of them. It is precisely because I accept two Dummettian principles that the task of outlining a substantive theory of content is so demanding: the principle that a theory of Thoughts must be a theory of things which determine truth values, and the principle that a theorist must give an account of how the semantical properties he attributes are specifically manifested in thought and action. The position I will be defending is one of manifestationism without verificationism.

PART I

TRUTH AND CONTENT

2

A General Conjecture:
The Observational Case

There are two dimensions to the characterization of the propositional content of a given sentence or of a given mental state. On the one hand, there is a dimension which carries information about such matters as the conditions which may lead a thinker to accept such a content, and its consequences in thought once accepted. On the other hand, there is the truth condition of the content. An investigation of the first dimension might have as its goal an adequate description of the conditions under which certain contents are in fact accepted; or it might have as its goal a correct statement of normative conditions relating to those contents. I will be concerned here only with normative conditions: henceforth, by an "acceptance condition" of a given content, I mean a correct statement of a normative condition concerning acceptance of that content. An acceptance condition may state a condition under which a particular content ought rationally to be accepted, but that is not the only sort of acceptance condition. A statement of what, rationally, must be accepted if a given content is judged can equally be an acceptance condition in this sense. A question then immediately arises about the relation between these two dimensions which characterize content: what, in general, *is* the relation between a content's acceptance conditions and its truth condition?

I will be arguing in support of, though will by no means

prove, the conjecture that there is a conception of a content's acceptance conditions on which those acceptance conditions determine its truth condition. More specifically, I will be arguing in support of this *Conjecture*:

> There is a class of contents whose truth conditions are directly determined by certain of their acceptance conditions; the truth conditions of contents outside this class are determined ultimately by their relations to contents inside this initial class.

In this Chapter I will argue for the Conjecture in the case of certain observational contents; in the next I will argue for it in connection with certain universally quantified contents.

The first part of the Conjecture as displayed would be instantly endorsed by someone who holds that truth itself is to be elucidated as some form of ideal fulfilment of evidential conditions: in fact such a theorist will hold that the first part covers all cases. But that is not the way in which I will be arguing for the Conjecture. I will not on the one hand be stating the acceptance conditions of a content solely in terms of the actions of a being with powers greater than, or different from, our own: such an approach is powerless by itself to illuminate the relations between *our* acceptance of a content and its truth conditions. Nor on the other hand will I be paring down truth conditions in some way which guarantees in advance of investigation of any particular type of content that the Conjecture must be correct. I will not be presupposing an anti-realistic theory of truth. What I will be supporting is something which has in a full theory to be established by detailed argument about the actual acceptance conditions and the pretheoretical truth condition of the content, in the absence of independent reasons for thinking these are defective. Such an argument has to be given for each type of content in our conceptual repertoire. We may, though, hope that there are some general forms of argument that can be used for several different types of content in establishing the Conjecture.

We need to avoid trivialization of the Conjecture. It would be trivialized if we allow as an acceptance condition of 'Men are mortal' the condition that it ought to be accepted only if men really are mortal: and who is to gainsay the correctness of that normative requirement? The relevant acceptance conditions must then be further restricted – to those for which we have an immediate account of how a thinker can manifest the fact that he is following its norms, rather than some others. Whenever I give acceptance conditions for a particular content, I will aim to show that this further restriction is met. If the Conjecture is correct, of course, conformity to the norms of an acceptance condition which does use the truth condition outright can after all be manifested: but on the conception I will be outlining, the account of manifestation of such conformity proceeds *via* acceptance conditions for which we have a direct account of manifestation. That is, grasp of a truth condition is manifested by a thinker's manifesting his conformity to certain normative acceptance conditions in making his judgements for reasons: and these normative conditions in turn determine the truth condition.

The acceptance conditions I will be discussing commonly concern in part the world external to the head of the thinker; they will not be restricted to psychological states which have no implications for the subject's environment. So these acceptance conditions for a content should not be identified with what many who have used the notion would call the conceptual role of a mental state with that content.[1] On such an internal notion of conceptual role, the conceptual role of a state is concerned only with that state's relations to stimulation, to behaviour and to other internal states: it is immediate that such internal conceptual roles will by themselves in almost all cases fail to determine truth conditions, which will generally concern the external world. The project of elucidating the acceptance conditions which will concern me and the project of elucidating internal conceptual role are distinct from one another.

---

[1] H. Field 'Logic, Meaning and Conceptual Role' *Journal of Philosophy* 74 (1977), pp. 379–409, at p. 380; B. Loar 'Conceptual Role and Truth Conditions' *Notre Dame Journal of Formal Logic* 23 (1982), pp. 272–83, at p. 280; see further C. McGinn 'The structure of content' in *Thought and Object* (Oxford: O.U.P., 1982), ed. A. Woodfield, S. Schiffer, 'Intention-based semantics', *Notre Dame Journal, ibid.*, pp. 119–56, and also the latter's 'Truth and The Theory of Content', in *Meaning and Understanding* (Berlin: de Gruyter, 1981), ed. H. Parret and J. Bouvresse. For a conceptual role theory which is not internal in the sense of the text, see G. Harman, 'Conceptual Role Semantics', *Notre Dame Journal of Formal Logic* 23 (1982) pp. 242–56.

The two projects may, of course, be surrounded by claims which do make the projects conflict. A theorist of internal conceptual role who says that it is *only* at the level of internal conceptual role that the dimension of content which captures acceptance conditions can be characterised would certainly be saying something competing with the account I will be offering.[2] So equally would a theorist – of either internal or wider conceptual role – who claims that insofar as he can make sense of the possibility at all, the determination of truth conditions by evidential or other acceptance conditions is a trivial matter, not something needing argument for each particular type of content.[3] Before we can assess those further claims, we need to know more about the position they exclude: here I will elaborate a notion of an acceptance condition and its relation to truth conditions which do conform to the Conjecture.

We take first contents in which an observational concept is predicated in the present tense of an object demonstratively presented in perception: we will be concerned with cases in which the object is of such a size that it can, in our actual circumstances, be determined by perceiving the object whether or not it falls under the observational concept. Such contents or Thoughts would be expressed in English by 'that block is cubic', 'this plate is oval', 'that surface is blue'; but possession of attitudes to these contents is not necessarily restricted to creatures who have a language. Concepts are here taken as constituents of contents. So they are conceived as conforming to a Fregean condition on informativeness, a version of the condition which for Frege would correspondingly have governed the senses of predicative words: if the content 'An object is φ if and only if it is ψ' is potentially informative, then φ and ψ are distinct concepts. If we do not cut at least this finely,

---

[2] For a statement of something which would be a consequence of this further claim, see Loar, *op. cit.*: 'I doubt that on *any* use theory (anything on which meaning is a matter of rules, verification procedures, etc.) whatever constitutes a sentence's meaning would explain or vindicate assigning our preferred truth-conditions to that sentence' (*op. cit.*, pp. 282–3). Loar's more detailed views, on which that formulation would be qualified for observational beliefs, are given in his *Mind and Meaning* (Cambridge: C.U.P., 1981), esp. Chapter 8.

[3] Harman is a representative of this second attitude: cp. his 'Conceptual Role Semantics', *op. cit.*

we will leave out too much that is distinctive of cognitive phenomena.

Contents within the chosen range have the following components. In the first component, the perceived object is presented in a certain way W in perception; some concept F – 'block', 'plate', 'surface' – is commonly used in individuating the object presented; and there is the presented object itself, x say. So the first component can be captured in the notation $[W,F(\ )_x]$. Second, there is the observational concept φ. Third is the time, t say, given as the present in these contents: we can write this component of the content $[now_t]$. The whole content 'that F is φ' is $[W,F(\ )_x]\hat{\ }[\varphi]\hat{\ }[now_t]$: here '$\hat{\ }$'stands for the component-forming operation on constituents of contents which corresponds, in this simple case, to concatenation on linguistic expressions for those constituents.[4]

If someone judges one of these contents, what commitments does he thereby incur? In asking this, I am asking about one particular sort of acceptance condition. In particular, I am asking about the spectrum of nondefeasible commitments attributable to a thinker in virtue of his judging just that content, as opposed to commitments which may be incurred given auxiliary hypotheses by which the thinker connects that content with others. They are commitments associated with the content itself, in that we cannot make sense of the idea that someone is judging that very content but does not in one way or another incur these commitments. So these commitments may also be labelled *canonical*. As a first approximation for the spectrum of canonical commitments we might try:

(C)   The spectrum of canonical commitments of one who judges a content at t 'That block is cubic' is that: for any position from which he were to perceive the block at t in normal external conditions when his perceptual mechanisms are minimally functioning, he would experience the

---

[4] In what follows, nothing essentially turns on having x and t themselves as constituents (albeit under modes of presentation) of the content. Any pairing of a context together with something which, applied to the content, yields x and t can be adapted to the purposes below. The constituent $[\varphi]$ could also be further decomposed. The square brackets around the 'φ' are only for stylistic uniformity in the formal representation.

block from that relative position as cubic, or as a cubic object would be perceived from that relative position.[5]

In a fuller theory this specification of the canonical commitments, like that for any other type of content, should be derivable from a specification of the contribution to canonical commitments made by the constituents of the given content. The idea behind this first effort is that in perceiving the block as cubic, a subject can confirm that one of the many instances of the displayed universally quantified condition is true. In the context of auxiliary hypotheses about what happens when he moves, the other instances may be inductively confirmed. What the thinker has to do to keep track of the object as he or it moves depends in part on how it is presented to him in perception, in part on its kind. Not only does the thinker actually confirm in his perceptual experience only a fragment of the spectrum of commitments; he does not know infallibly that he has confirmed that fragment, since he does not know infallibly about the state of his perceptual mechanisms or environmental conditions and moving around the object in any case takes time. But infallibility aside, instances of this spectrum of canonical commitments can be confirmed. The thinker need not, of course, have these specifications of canonical commitments consciously in mind, or be capable of formulating them. What matters is that they correctly describe his commitments. That they *are* his commitments will be shown by the circumstances in which he is willing to withdraw a judgement of the content. Suppose a thinker is not questioning the normality of his environment, nor the operation of his perceptual mechanisms: then the pattern of his actual and counterfactual acceptances and rejections of 'That block is cubic' in rational response to his perceptual experiences can

[5] This applies only to monadic observational predications of perceptually presented objects. A variant account is needed even for some observational relations, particularly when one of their terms is the perceiver himself. It can hardly be required for fulfilment of the canonical commitments of a first-person thought 'I am in front of that (perceptually presented) house' that if I were in any different nearby position, I would still have an experience as of myself being in front of the house. The requirement would have to concern the perceived relation from other positions between the place I was previously located and the house.

make it reasonable to ascribe to him the spectrum of commitments in (C).

If (C) or something in the same spirit is correct, a thinker capable of judging 'That block is cubic' will be capable of responding differentially in his judgements to the line between experiences which represent a given thing as cubic (or a way a cubic thing would look from certain angles) and those which represent it as having some other shape. It does not at all follow from this that the thinker must have *concepts* of all these different shapes which must be mentioned in specifying the content of these experiences to the division within which he is sensitive. The various contents relating to the shape of a presented object when it is seen from different angles will be given by what Evans called *non-conceptual content*[6]: more specifically, it is given by what I elsewhere call *analogue content*.[7]

Two thinkers may vary greatly in their inductive boldness, but may still judge the very same content. The bolder thinker may require much less than the more timid thinker in the way of evidence that the canonical commitments of one of our observational contents are fulfilled. But the commitments he incurs, on a narrower evidential base, are the same as those of the timid thinker in judging the same content: for these observational contents, I will be arguing that this identity of commitments is what makes it the case that they are judging the same content.

In the case of the concept of being cubic, and other concepts of primary qualities, there is no one sense modality such that possession of these concepts demands a specified sensitivity to perceptions in that particular sense modality. Both a visual and a tactile experience can represent something in one's hand as being cubic, or two nearby edges as parallel, or as pointed. What matters here is the relative order of the modal operator and the quantifier. There is no modality such that for

---

[6]*The Varieties of Reference* (Oxford: O.U.P., 1982), especially pp. 122–9, 154–60. Unlike Evans, though, I hold that the representational nonconceptual content of perception does enter the content of some judgements: see the work cited in the next footnote.

[7]See my Inaugural Address in the *Proceedings of the Aristotelian Society Supplementary Volume* **60** (1986).

possession of these concepts sensitivity to perceptions in that modality is necessary: but it is necessary that there be perceptions in some modality such that there be a certain rational sensitivity of judgements containing the concept to those perceptions, if the concept is to be observational. My discussion will mainly mention visual experience: but it will, in the case of an observational concept of a primary quality, be sufficient for possession of it that the conditions mentioned for visual experience be correspondingly fulfilled for experience in some other sense modality. Primary qualities can be accessed through different modalities precisely because they are concepts of objective properties whose nature is independent of any particular form of sense experience.

This objectivity is in fact not fully captured in that first approximation to the spectrum of canonical commitments. We can conceive of something which changes shape as a normal perceiver moves around it; and we can conceive of its doing so in such a way that from any position it looks cubic to the perceiver, even though it never is in fact really cubic. The full spectrum of canonical commitments offered in the first approximation could be fulfilled without exhausting the real commitments of one who judges the content. The real commitments exclude the state of affairs just described.

It is not right to say that the point is already accommodated by the appeal to normal conditions in the first approximation. Consider a curious sceptic who maintains that things around us do often change shape as we move around them. Can we really answer him by saying 'But these are normal conditions we are in, so your scepticism is unintelligible'? On the contrary, there is no problem in understanding (as opposed to believing) this sceptical hypothesis. What, in the case of the concept of being cubic, has been omitted from the canonical commitments is this: it has to be the object's *actual* shape in present circumstances which is responsible in the counterfactual circumstances mentioned for the perceptual experiences. What happens in counterfactual circumstances in which the object has a different shape from that it actually possesses is irrelevant to the fulfilment of *these* commitments. The judgement that the presented object is cubic must be withdrawn if it becomes clear that the actual shape is not responsible for the relevant experiences, even if all the counterfactuals in the first approximation are true – as they could be under the curious sceptic's hypothesis. (Equally, if a (surface) colour concept is predicated of a surface, some actual property of the surface of the object must in the counterfactual circumstances cause the experiences mentioned in the canonical commitments.) It also matters that in the improved statement of the canonical commitments, we say that it is the object's actual shape which is responsible for the experiences, rather than saying that it is the fact that the object is cubic which is so responsible. The latter, though true, trivializes the Conjecture: the former does not.

What is a "minimally functioning" perceiver? Is it a necessary condition of a subject's being a minimally functioning perceiver that if his experience represents his environment as being a certain way, it is so? This matching requirement is too strong. Someone may wonder this: 'I know my perceptual mechanisms are in order, and the lighting is normal, but are those things which I see as square perhaps not really square?' This is a coherent speculation. A philosophical account of a minimally functioning perceiver must accommodate the fact, so familiar to psychologists and artists, that, for example, even with the normal behaviour of light, many different irregular trapezoids can cause a visual experience as of something square in the environment.[8] These different shapes have in common that they cause the same pattern of retinal stimulation. If we imposed the matching requirement on minimally functioning perceivers, our wondering subject would be wondering something *a priori* incoherent, which he is not.

Rather than impose the matching requirement, we can proceed thus. A description of things in the environment of a subject is *in the projection class* of a given pattern of retinal stimulation just in case the existence of things in the environment falling under that description could, with the normal behaviour of light, be part of the causal explanation of the occurrence of an instance of that pattern of retinal stimulation. A description of the form 'A door of such-and-

<hr>

[8] See, for instance, J. Hochberg, *Perception*, second edition (Englewood Cliffs, N.J.: Prentice-Hall, 1978), Figure 28, p. 55.

such shape, colour and texture at so-and-so orientation and distance relative to the subject' is in the projection class of the pattern of retinal stimulation which you normally receive when you look at such a door. That same class will also have as a member a description of a carefully painted facade at a very different angle which contains no real door or any salient segment which is door-shaped, but which with the normal behaviour of light produces the same pattern of retinal stimulation. With this notion, we can then say that a subject is a minimally functioning perceiver only if two conditions are met when he has a perceptual experience in normal external circumstances: (i) the description under which the experience represents things in the environment as falling is in the projection class of the pattern of retinal stimulation which causes the experience, and (ii) suitable relations of causal explanation obtain between the occurrence of that pattern and the experience (the details do not matter here).[9] A minimally functioning perceiver will not necessarily be very efficient – he could be much less efficient than humans in many circumstances – but the following is true of any minimally functioning perceiver. By viewing an object from different positions, he obtains a class of descriptions of what is in his environment which are in the projection classes of *all* the successive patterns of retinal stimulation. This will in general be a much narrower set than the projection class of any one such pattern. In particular, a description of the environment as containing an irregular trapezoid will not be in the projection class of all the successive patterns when a square is viewed from different angles. That is why views from different positions still matter. Similarly, features of objects causally inoperative in producing experiences when the subject is at one location may come into their own when he moves.[10]

In the statement (C) of canonical commitments, the whole universally quantified condition beginning 'For any position

---

[9] Note that someone subject to a geometrical illusion is *not* a minimally functioning perceiver under this definition: the concept is not at all the same as that of a normally functioning perceiver.

[10] These examples and points substantially modify the claims about differential explanation and the definition of perception in my *Holistic Explanation* (Oxford: O.U.P., 1979), Chapter 2.

. . .' is to be understood as falling within the scope of the thinker's commitment in judging 'That block is cubic'. Suppose the thinker continues to believe the content 'That block is cubic' in the face of one of his experiences of the block which represents it as curved, say. Then he is committed to believing that either external conditions are not normal or that his perceptual mechanisms are not functioning properly. Again, he does not need to be able to formulate this explicitly: that he has incurred these commitments will be shown in the actual and counterfactual ways he tries to make his judgements coherent. There is no question of the thinker being capable of such observational judgements without his also being capable of first-person thoughts, judgements about his location, and much else: we have here a substantial local holism to which I will return in Chapter 4.

So much for preliminaries. How does this bear on the relation between acceptance conditions and truth conditions? I claim that for contents of the sort which are our current concern:

(S.Obs)   For any such content, if all its canonical commitments are met, then it is true.

(S.Obs) is so called because it gives a sufficient condition for the truth of one of our observational contents. I also claim:

(N.Obs)   For any such content, if it is true, then all its canonical commitments are met.

– so called because it gives a necessary condition. If (S.Obs) and (N.Obs) are true, then for this restricted class of contents, certain acceptance conditions – the canonical commitments – determine the truth conditions. (S.Obs) ought to be the more controversial case. For any particular observational concept φ, one would argue for instances of (S.Obs) involving it by contraposition: remember that we are concerned here only with concepts φ such that as things actually are, it can be determined by perception of something whether it is φ. The argument for (S.Obs) is then that if external conditions are normal, anything which is not φ actually has a property which would, from some position, cause it not to be experienced by a minimally functioning perceiver as an observably φ thing would.[11] As promised, this argument does not proceed from some general prior identification of truth with ideal fulfilment of evidential conditions, but makes points specific to the kind of content in question. The argument is, for example, inapplicable altogether to concepts which do not possess the connections with perceptual experience distinctive of observational notions. It would also be inapplicable to any ways of thinking of a natural kind which do involve some perceptual component, but which require also a certain internal or theoretical constitution of its instances.[12]

The argument just given draws upon three notions concerning content without elucidating them. It takes for granted the conceptual content of experience. It also employs the idea of one external object rather than another being the one demonstratively presented and thought about. Finally, it simply uses the notion of the commitments being fulfilled, that is, true. These surely all need further elucidation, and they all – including the representational content of experience – need it by appeal to the relations between the thinker's states and external things. So the account of the relation between acceptance and truth which (S.Obs) and (N.Obs) give is partial. Nevertheless it matters that we can do it, for by giving it we fulfil the need to have an account which possesses what we can call *internal determinacy*. For it would be problematic if, even when we are allowed to help ourselves to what I have taken

---

[11] A more general argument relevant to instances of (S.Obs) concerning shape concepts could also be built from a striking theorem of Ullman's: see his paper 'The Interpretation of Structure from Motion', *Proc. Royal Soc. of London* B **203** (1979), pp. 405–26. He shows that three distinct orthographic views of four non-coplanar points on a rigid object suffice to determine its three dimensional shape (up to a reflection). An efficient perceptual system will exploit this fact: we should not expect a vast number of views to be needed to determine three dimensional shape.

[12] We have not established that the acceptance conditions determine the truth conditions even for all contents of our chosen observational form: for we were operating under the restriction that the object perceptually presented is one the applicability to which of the observational concept can be perceptually determined. The restriction is genuine: consider 'That star is spherical' judged by someone looking at a star in the night sky with the naked eye. To establish the Conjecture for all contents of this type would require arguments of a quite different sort, dealing with theoretical inferences to (for instance) shape in the very small or very large which play no part in the cases of the text. The considerations of Chapter 5 apply to grasp of shape in the very large and very small.

without earning, the truth conditions of these simple contents outstripped their acceptance conditions.[13]

We will sometimes regard as true a content 'If I were in the next room, it would still be the case that that (perceptually presented) table is rectangular' ([W, table( )$_x$]ˆ< being rectangular>ˆ[now$_t$]). This is not equivalent to 'If I were in the next room, a content of the form [W, table ( )$_\xi$]ˆ< being rectangular > ˆ[now$_\eta$] judged by me there would be true'. So how do we explain the role of our observational contents in such embeddings? In general, for each content of the form [W,F( )$_x$]ˆ[φ]ˆ[now$_t$] there is a corresponding *proposition* <x,P,t> consisting of the perceived object x, the property P presented by the observational concept φ in the content, and the time presented. This is a Russellian proposition in a sense emphasized by David Kaplan.[14] For the purposes of evaluating

---

[13] I have been oversimplifying for simplicity of exposition. In fact a thinker may withdraw a judgement that the presented object is cubic when he should not, *i.e.* he may make mistakes. We can consider someone who, when depth cues are virtually nonexistent, sees what is in fact a wire cube from an angle from which it appears thus:

We should make the relevant withdrawal conditions dependent upon the way the shape is thought of, and there is more than one distinctively perceptual way of thinking of the shape property of being cubic: see G. Hinton, 'Some Demonstrations of the Effects of Structural Descriptions in Mental Imagery' *Cognitive Science* 3 (1979), pp. 231–50. The canonical commitments of a given observational content containing a given shape concept should require withdrawal only when the subject enjoys views of the object *obviously not* one which would be presented by something falling under that concept. A mistaken withdrawal may be due to incorrect inference: such withdrawals should not be determinative of the canonical commitments of the content in question. After this modification, the thesis of this chapter must be this: the truth condition of an observational content is determined by the canonical commitments concerning perceptions of the object from relative positions from which it is obvious how something falling under the given concept would appear.

[14] See, for example, Russell's letter of 12 December 1904 to Frege: 'I believe that in spite of all its snowfields Mont Blanc itself is a component part of what is actually asserted in the proposition "Mont Blanc is more than 4000 metres high".' On Russell's theory, the mountain itself is a constituent of 'what is actually asserted'; in this quotation, Russell characteristically also uses 'proposition' for the linguistic expression too. Amongst his many writings on this topic, see David Kaplan's 'How to Russell a Frege-Church' *Journal of Philosophy* **72** (1975), pp. 716–29.

these counterfactuals, the truth of the content with respect to nonactual circumstances requires that the object x have property P at t, *i.e.* that its corresponding proposition be true. Unless there is some difficulty about which object and property are so presented, principles giving the canonical commitments of these contents will suffice, if we use the notion of the corresponding proposition, for the determination of what has to be the case for the content to be true in any arbitrary circumstance.

If the conjunction of (S.Obs) and (N.Obs) allows us to say that canonical commitments determine truth conditions, we can hardly deny that in the same sense truth conditions here determine canonical commitments. But this must not be misunderstood. (S.Obs) says that the *fulfilment* of the commitments ensures the *fulfilment* of the truth conditions, and (N.Obs) says the converse: neither (S.Obs) nor (N.Obs) says anything explicitly about uniqueness. In particular, (N.Obs) does not guarantee that associated with each truth condition, if (for the purposes of this paragraph only) that is taken in these examples as given merely by the ordered triple of an object, property and time (the Russellian proposition), there is associated a *unique* pattern of canonical commitments. (N.Obs) ensures only this: if the truth condition for a content obtains, the spectrum of commitments for that content are fulfilled. This is quite consistent with the nonexistence of a route back from reference to sense: for it can be informative to say of two spectra of commitments that the one is fulfilled if and only if the other is. So there can still be a unique content-determining association of a spectrum of canonical commitments with a given content. Thus suppose we could both feel heat and see it with infra-red vision. If the terms 'heat$_1$' and 'heat$_2$' are introduced for the physical properties presented in these two ways, the thought that something is hot$_1$ if and only if it is hot$_2$ can be informative. Correspondingly, consider the two thoughts that an object, presented in a given way, is hot$_1$ and that it is hot$_2$. The canonical commitments of the first thought are all fulfilled if and only if the canonical commitments of the second thought are: but this an *a posteriori* truth. The canonical commitments will indeed be uniquely determined by an object, property and time under suitable modes of presentation. But on the conception underlying this paper, that is unsurprising: for the conception is that a substantive theory of sense can be given by appealing to acceptance conditions, of which a specification of canonical commitments is but a special case.[15]

When the predicative component of one of our observational contents is a primary quality concept, the content is one that can be barely true, in Dummett's sense adapted to contents: for him, a barely true statement is one for which there is no nontrivial answer to the question 'What makes it true?'.[16] Dummett has also said that our model for knowledge of what it is for a statement capable of being barely true is the ability to use it to give a report of observation.[17] This may need qualification if we allow contents about the entities postulated by the physical sciences to be barely true: but for observational contents, what we have argued so far supports Dummett's claim. The point is not that whenever, for instance, a minimally functioning subject has an experience as of something cubic in normal external circumstances, his experience will be caused by the perceived object's being cubic: we have already seen that to be false. What *is* true is that the only property of the presented object which would explain its appearing cubic (or as a cubic object would) from an arbitrary relative local position is its being cubic. This feature may be unique to the primary quality observational contents; and it helps to explain how we can grasp one range of contents which can be barely true.

Two different thinkers may confirm, to their satsifaction, that the canonical commitments of a given observational content are fulfilled. But since each confirms that they are met in the case of his own experiences, the question arises how they can be judging exactly the same content. Why for instance are they not rather judging contents of the same kind? The determination of truth conditions by acceptance conditions

---

[15] A genuine question for further work is whether there is a corresponding uniqueness in the case of (S.Obs): that is the question of the indeterminacy of the association of truth conditions with acceptance conditions. For scepticism about determinacy on a rather different notion of evidential conditions and conceptual role, see Schiffer, 'Truth and the Theory of Content', *op. cit.*.

[16] See his 'What is a Theory of Meaning? (II)' in *Truth and Meaning*, ed. G. Evans and J. McDowell (Oxford: O.U.P., 1976), p. 89ff.

[17] *Ibid.* p. 95.

helps to answer this question. The truth condition, which concerns the actual, causally operative properties of the presented object, is not person-relative. If the commitments in (C) are fulfilled with respect to any one thinker's experience, they are fulfilled with respect to that of any other thinker: it makes no difference which minimally functioning perceiver is in question. In arguing this, we are arguing for the fulfilment of a condition of adequacy on an acceptance-condition account of content which must always be met, *viz.*: if the content-determining acceptance conditions for a content are in some way thinker-relative, while its truth conditions are not, we must be able to establish that if the acceptance conditions are met for any one thinker, then they are met for every thinker.

There would be several other consequences of the determination of truth conditions by canonical commitments. One would be that a theorist who aims to individuate content by certain acceptance conditions (including canonical commitments) could consistently accept Dummett's arguments that a content (a Thought) is essentially something which, together with the world, determines a truth value.[18] Dummett's arguments suggest that it is an adequacy condition on a theory of sense that it treat contents (Thoughts) as essentially determiners of truth values, given the way the world is. If acceptance conditions do determine truth conditions, then a theory which uses acceptance conditions to individuate content can meet this adequacy condition. Another consequence concerns the claim that the achievement of understanding of a language, or grasp of certain contents, is in part a matter of acquiring a suitable rational sensitivity to acceptance conditions (which may include evidential conditions). This claim need not be competing with, but would actually entail, the thesis that these achievements are equally describable as the attainment of grasp, in a particular way, of the truth conditions of the contents.[19] This makes it important to ask whether some form of the present model might not be adapted to other types of content. One reason this question matters is that this treatment of the

---

[18] *The Interpretation of Frege's Philosophy* (London: Duckworth, 1981), p. 47.

[19] For a sharply contrasting view, see B. Loar, 'Conceptual Role and Truth Conditions', *op.cit.* p. 276ff. and especially fn 4.

relatively simple observational contents suggests an account distinct from Dummett's of how grasp of a truth condition can be manifested. The general argument Dummett has given for anti-realism starts from the following thesis: that the content of a sentence is determined by the class of recognizable situations with respect to which it would be acknowledged as true and the class of recognizable situations with respect to which it would be recognized as false. He is surely right in saying that on such a conception of the determination of content, grasp of a content which, it is alleged, can be unrecognizably true becomes highly problematic. The conception can apparently be formulated without a commitment to the behaviourism which Dummett has sometimes seemed to endorse: so rejecting behaviourism does not automatically defuse this argument for anti-realism. The present treatment of observational concepts, however, has supplied an account of manifestation of grasp of a truth condition *without* using the notion of recognizing that the truth condition obtains. Rather, I have tried to say how, for each one of a family of commitments of a content, the thinker can manifest that it is one of his commitments in judging the content. This family of commitments then determines the truth condition, without apparently any need on the theorist's part to employ the notion of the thinker's recognizing the truth condition as obtaining. Now of course Dummett has always said that use of the notion of a truth condition coinciding with the classical one is unobjectionable for present tense observational contents. But it is not obvious that the scope of the commitment model is restricted to anti-realistically acceptable cases. In the next Chapter, we address the question 'Can the commitment model be applied elsewhere to give an account of grasp of contents which transcend verification?'.

3

Universal Quantification

The observational contents we considered in Chapter 2 are a very special case. But the relation between truth and acceptance conditions there is an instance of a more general form. The more general form is this: for each content there is a spectrum of commitments such that the content is true if and only if all those commitments are fulfilled. In the observational case these commitments involved perceptions which represented the world as being a certain way, a way systematically linked to the main concept of the content; but for other contents the correlating operation which determines the commitments from the content may be different. So one way in which we could generalize the initial model of the relations between truth and acceptance to a new, non-observational range of contents would be this:

> There is some operation C such that for each content p in the range:
> (i) $C(p)$ gives the canonical commitments of p, and
> (ii) p is true if and only if all the conditions in $C(p)$ obtain.

While one range of contents may be individuated by their canonical commitments, another range may be individuated by their canonically *committing* conditions: that is, by their canonical grounds rather than their canonical consequences.

For a range of contents individuated by their canonical grounds, we can say:

There is some operation G such that for each content p in the range:
(i) $G(p)$ gives the canonical grounds of p, and
(ii) p is true if and only if some condition in $G(p)$ obtains.

That a content has certain canonical grounds will be shown in the conditions a thinker takes as sufficient for its holding.

A more refined version of each of these models could accommodate some dependence, in the determination of the truth condition, on the attitudes of the individual thinker. Provided that the nature of this dependence is uniformly given from the content p, this need not in any fundamental way make truth conditions person-relative. On one way of refining the commitment model, for instance, there would be an additional operation B:

There are operations C and B such that for each content p in the range and for each thinker x:
(i) $C(p)$ gives the canonical commitments of p, and
(ii) p is true if and only if all the conditions in $C(p)$ and all the conditions in $B(p, x)$ obtain.

I will give an example of such a model later. One can envisage many less restrictive variations on this theme.

Our question now is: can some form of one of these schematic models be applied to contents which are universal objectual quantifications 'All F's are G' ($\forall x(Fx, Gx)$)?[1]

In the spirit of Ramsey, we might try to build a theory around the idea that one who believes that all F things are G is disposed, given as a premise a thought that m is F, to infer that m is G.[2] A theory built in this spirit must solve two problems. The first is that the theory must explain how quantificational

---

[1] The reasons for preferring the binary notation in parentheses to the standard '$\forall x(Fx \to Gx)$' are summarized in M. Davies, *Meaning, Quantification, Necessity* (London: Routledge and Kegan Paul, 1981), pp. 123–36.

[2] '$(x).\varphi x$ expresses an inference we are at any time prepared to make': *The Foundations of Mathematics* (London: Routledge and Kegan Paul, 1931), p. 238.

contents embed within more complex operators. On this first problem, the theorist can say the following. Suppose the inferential disposition of one who believes that all F's are G has been satisfactorily characterized. We can ask what condition has to hold in the world for exercise of this disposition never to lead to false belief. This will be the resultant truth condition for the content: and this truth condition can be input, in the extensional cases, to which other operators are applied when a quantification is embedded in more complex contents.[3] This is an adaptation of a tactic already adopted in the observational case. The second problem is that as the theory stands, the disposition it offers would also be possessed by a thinker whose quantification 'All F's are G's' has the truth condition that all the objects of which he has, or will have, modes of presentation of any sort in his repertoire are G. The theorist has to offer an account which uniquely determines objectual quantification over all objects of the given kind.

Accounts of quantification rarely address the question of what makes a subject's thought one containing unrestricted objectual quantification, rather than some analogue for thought of substitutional quantification. Evans, for instance, in an illuminating discussion wrote 'the proposition that some F is G is conceived to be such that it would be rendered true by the truth of some proposition of the form "δ is G", where δ is a fundamental Idea of an F.'[4] It is no objection to this that the phrase 'some proposition of the form . . .' is within the scope of 'conceived to be such that . . .': Evans was not trying to give an eliminative analysis of grasp of existential quantification, but rather a principle describing it. But there need be no Idea or mode of presentation δ in the thinker's present or future repertoire which verifies a true existential quantification which the thinker judges.[5] If we are puzzled about the nature of mastery of unrestricted quantification over objects, the statement that such a quantification is conceived to be true in virtue

---

[3] Here the theorist departs from Ramsey, who seems to have held that quantified sentences do not express propositions in just the same sense in which their purely singular instances do: cp. *The Foundations of Mathematics*, pp. 238–42.

[4] *The Varieties of Reference*, p. 108.

[5] As Evans noted: *ibid.*, pp. 108–9.

of a condition which involves unrestricted universal quantification over fundamental Ideas of those objects should not totally remove our puzzlement. We might be tempted to say that we are considering an ideal thinker such that for each F, there is some Idea or mode of presentation of it in his repertoire. But then we must explain how our actual, non-ideal thought achieves the same truth conditions as those possessed by the thoughts of the ideal thinker; and in doing so we must also explain our grasp of the thought 'For each F, there is some Idea of it in the ideal thinker's repertoire'.

This problem is of course not special to the universal and existential quantifiers. It arises for any second-level operator whose truth conditions ineliminably involve the full range of objects falling under some concept: it arises equally for the definite description operator, and for such second-level predicates as 'rare', as it occurs in 'Albinos are rare'. What we must give is an elucidation of the phenomenon which Dummett characterizes by saying 'We understand the universally quantified statement because we have, as it were, a *general* grasp of the totality which constitutes the domain of quantification – we, as it were, survey it in thought as a whole. . .'.[6]

We seek an account of grasp of objectual universal quantification in terms of canonical commitments. The account should be one which determines the objectual truth conditions, and thus explains the remarkable fact that humans are capable of grasping a content which requires for its truth something about *all* objects of a given kind. Now there will certainly be differences, accessible to a radical interpreter, between one whose quantifications are objectual and one whose quantifications are substitutional. The empirical conditions which make it reasonable to judge an objectual universal quantification are much more demanding than those making it reasonable to judge a substitutional quantification.[7] On some

---

[6] *Frege: Philosophy of Language* (London: Duckworth, Second Edition, 1981), p. 517.

[7] Here I assume that all the terms in the substitution class denote. If they do not, there will still be other empirical differences between quantifiers read in each of the two ways.

definitions of validity, there will also be differences in the logic to which the two quantifiers conform.[8] But these indisputable points do not give us quite what we were seeking: they either come too late, or they raise the same problems. We are asking for a certain form of account which explains how it is that a content can concern all objects. Given that it does, its doing so will have the mentioned consequences which differentiate it from substitutional quantifications. But these particular consequences do not constitute an account of what makes it the case that the content does range over all objects: it has certainly not been shown that they determine the truth condition.

On the other hand, some *ideal* radical interpretation procedure for identifying specifically objectual universal quantification, rather than those particular features differentiating the objectual from the substitutional, might be proposed as supplying what we seek. The ideal procedure would specify what, at the level of facts accessible to the radical interpreter, has to be the case for someone to mean universal objectual quantification by something. If our initial Conjecture of the previous section is correct, it is indeed reasonable to expect that an ideal radical interpretation procedure for such quantification and an account of its canonical commitments or grounds will be equivalent: they are just accounts from different perspectives, the internal and the external, of what makes it the

[8] Kripke observes that, if we define validity for substitutional formulae in a way which takes as the range of substitution classes arbitrary sets of expressions of the appropriate category, then substitutional validity and classical objectual validity coincide: a formula is substitutionally valid iff it is classically valid. ('Is There a Problem about Substitutional Quantification?', in *Truth and Meaning*, ed. G. Evans and J. McDowell (Oxford: O.U.P., 1976), at p. 36.) This is not, though, the only definition of validity possible; and there are also ways of elaborating the idea of something being accepted as a law which would be tied to another definition of validity. In particular, as Davies notes, if the substitution classes quantified over in the definition of validity are restricted to those containing expressions already in the language, a wider class of formulae is valid. ('A Note on Substitutional Quantification', *Nous* 14 (1980), pp. 619–22). In a language whose only individual constants are a and b, and whose only term-forming functors are f and g, any instance of the schema $[Fa \& Fb \& \forall x F(f(x)) \& \forall x F(g(x))] \rightarrow \forall x Fx$ is valid under that altered definition. A reflective thinker who is using substitutional quantification will accept all instances of this schema; a thinker using objectual quantification will not do so. There are also differences in the relation of logical consequence on the altered definition of validity. (J.M. Dunn and N.D. Belnap, 'The Substitution Interpretation of the Quantifiers', *Nous* 2 (1968), p. 177.)

case that a thinker is judging one content rather than another. But such an ideal radical interpretation procedure which says something specific about universal unrestricted objectual quantification we still do not have – in effect it is, from a different perspective, what I am trying to supply.

Let us initially confine our attention to unrestricted quantification over physical objects which exist at the present time. Each such object is individuated by its current location and its kind. If we can explain quantification over all places, we can explain quantification over all such objects: for all F's to be G it has to be that for every place the F (if any) at that place is G.

What is our conception of the range of unrestricted variables over places? I suggest that it is governed, *inter alia*, by two principles. (i) It is closed under such functions as those given by phrases of the form 'the place bearing spatial relation R to place π', when these functions are applied to places already in the domain. Of course in the case of some relations R, there will be no place bearing R to a given place already in the domain – for instance if the universe is finite and bearing R to π entails the relation of being more than a certain distance away from π. But *if* there is such a place, it is in the range of the unrestricted variables over places. (ii) Understanding unrestricted quantification over places does not consist in the existence of a finite list of relations of which the understander appreciates that the range of places is closed under just those relations. Rather, the understanding is open-ended: for any new spatial relations with which he is presented, the understander will take the range of places as closed under those relations. This allows for arbitrary fineness of discrimination of smaller regions, and for the discrimination of distinct places at great distances.[9]

---

[9] This should not necessarily be equated with the range being indefinitely extensible, in Dummett's sense. (A concept is indefinitely extensible if 'for any definite characterization of it, there is a natural extension of this characterization, which yields a more inclusive concept': *Truth and Other Enigmas* (London: Duckworth, 1978), p. 195ff.) If we are allowed to use the real numbers in the specification of the spatial relations, there will be characterizations of the range of places which are maximally inclusive. There may be, though, philosophical reasons for holding that the totality of real numbers cannot itself be explained except by using some indefinitely extensible notion – perhaps 'concept true or false of natural numbers'. So the thesis that the range of unrestricted quantification over places is either indefinitely extensible or has to be elucidated using some indefinitely extensible notion is still in the field.

According to what we will call the Revised Account, to judge that all (physical, currently existent) F's are G is to be committed to judging, should the question arise, any instance of the schema (1):

(1)　If there is an F at the place (if any) bearing R to π, it is G.[10]

Here any term replacing 'π' denotes a place already thought of as being in the domain of places. The judgemental disposition in question may be described as open-ended, in a sense corresponding to that in which the conception of the range of relations under which the domain of places is closed is open-ended. That is, it is enough for a thinker's now judging that all F's are G that he now judges something which precisely commits him, when presented with what he takes to be a new spatial relation, to accept the corresponding instance of (1). He need not now know of all such relations. The phrase 'what he takes to be' matters here. A thinker may believe there are spatial relations other than those there actually are: without irrationality, he may be disposed to judge any instance of (1) involving a real spatial relation, without judging that all F's are G. Conversely, if he believes of something which is a genuine spatial relation that it is no such thing, he may correspondingly judge the universal quantification without having that disposition with respect to everything which really is a spatial relation.[11]

The Revised Account preserves an attractive feature of the original Ramseyan theory. It offers an explanation of why there is such a gap between judging that $\forall x(Fx, Gx)$ and judging that $Ga \ \& \ Gb \ \& \dots \& \ Gt$, where $a \dots t$ are in fact all the F's there are. To accept that last conjunction is by no means to have the general and indefinitely extensible disposition required by the Revised Account if one is to be judging the universal

---

[10] In the special case of generalizations of the form 'All *places* are G', (1) should be replaced by 'The place (if any) bearing R to π is G'.

[11] A thinker may consistently judge both that all F's are G, and that *if* there is an F in such-and-such region, then it is *not* G. But this does not contradict the account built around (1). On the Revised Account, there is no inconsistency either in this thinker or in our description of him. On the Revised Account, he is committed to believing both 'If there is an F in such-and-such region, then it is G' and 'If there is an F in such-and-such region, it is not G'. Hence on that account he is committed to believing there is no F in such-and-such region; and indeed he is so committed.

generalization. Indeed there is no particular singular mode of presentation such that a thinker must, in virtue of judging a universal generalization, already have it in his conceptual repertoire: this is as it should be, and it is a second virtue of any neo-Ramseyan account.

If all the canonical commitments, according to the Revised Account, for 'All F's are G' are fulfilled, must it then be true that all F's are G? Not quite: for the canonical commitments concerned the *recognized* spatial relations, which may diverge from the real spatial relations. All we can say is that if all those canonical commitments are fulfilled, all the F's the thinker *believes* to exist will be G. But let us remember the refined version of the commitment model, which contained a clause about $B(p)$, an operation which may concern the individual thinker's attitudes. It is true that if all the canonical commitments for 'All F's are G' are fulfilled, *and* that the thinker is disposed to recognize a relation as a spatial relation just in case it really is a spatial relation, then all F's will be G. This is the promised instance of the refined version of the model.

These points presuppose that every place within the range of the thinker's quantifiers is individuated by some extension of the thinker's conceptual resources for specifying spatial relations. These extensions will involve the application of mathematics to the real world. If someone believes that a subject's quantifications sometimes include in their range objects not capturable this way, we can ask him what features of that subject's thought make this fact manifest. If he can cite such features, the strategy of one who proposes the Revised Account will be to adapt his theory to accommodate those features. If no such features can be cited, he will be sceptical that any objects which ought to be captured remain uncaptured by his account.

Have I been cheating? At two points, I have used second-level objectual operators in giving a content: and I have presupposed a grasp of that content by the thinker when explaining the commitments of his universal quantifications. First, we exploited the equivalence, for predicates of material objects, of 'All F's are G' with 'For every place, the F (if any) at that place is G'. Then there was also the occurrence of 'There is . . .' in (1). But this accusation of cheating presupposes that the enterprise in which I have been engaged has reductive aspirations of a kind which in fact it need not possess. I have been trying to show how the canonical commitments of a universal quantification illuminatingly determine its classical truth condition. This remains a reasonable goal even in the context of an account of universal quantification in which such quantification is used within the scope of the attitudes of the thinker whose grasp of the notion is in question. In such a context, the present account is indeed incomplete. Consider the property of a second-level operator picked out as follows: one takes the conjunction of all the canonical commitments of a universal quantification, and replaces throughout occurrences of the universal quantifier within propositional attitude contexts by an appropriately typed variable V; if the result is ___V___, the property we will be concerned with is picked out by the term $\lambda V[$___V___$]$, which is a property of second-level properties. Now the account is incomplete because one ought in addition to show one of two things which I have not shown: either that universal quantification is the only operator with the property $\lambda V[$___V___$]$, or that there are additional constraints on universal quantification, and these together with the property $\lambda V[$___V___$]$ are jointly possessed only by universal quantification. However, in either case the account in terms of commitments can be an essential part of an account of mastery of universal quantification.[12]

[12] It might be thought that the reductive aspirations could in any case be met by careful use of restricted quantification. The idea would be to make use of this fact: that the equivalence 'All F's are G iff for any place π, the F at π is G' still holds if its contained 'the' is given a restricted range systematically dependent upon and including the place π; (1) can be modified similarly. But even if the reductive constraint were accepted, this move would not meet it: in grasping an explicitly restricted quantification, which still contains unrestricted objectual variables, one has to have some grasp of the latter variables' unrestricted range. If one wanted to conform to the requirements of one type of reduction – a reduction not of concepts but of concept-mastery – one might offer a different reply: this would be the reply that each canonical commitment of a universal quantification can be stated in a way understanding of which does not require grasp of unrestricted quantification. Any one such statement would involve a universal quantifier whose domain is narrower than that of our unrestricted quantifiers (over material objects), rather than one containing explicit restrictions specified using unrestricted variables. It would of course not be the same such quantifier for every commitment: in fact infinitely many would be needed to verify the totality of modal claims made by the envisaged reductionist. But there is no reason to believe that in the general case we have to be able to go even this far towards meeting the demands of the reductionist.

The Revised Account may be contrasted with what we can call *relocation* theories. Relocation theories try to explain acceptance of $\forall x(Fx, Gx)$ in terms of conditionals the thinker actually accepts about the properties of F's he would encounter at other places. Suppose the relocation theorist says that to believe the present-tense 'All F's are G' is to accept such conditionals as (2):

(2)   If I travel north for a day, and there learn something of the form 'The so-and-so here is F', that F thing will also be G.

Does the relocation theory give as commitments only those conditionals whose antecedents concern a place a subject could, consistently with the laws of nature, travel to; or is there no such restriction? If there is no such restriction, we have to suppose that one who judges that all F's are G's is committed to counterfactuals concerning what would happen if he were at a place he could reach only by travelling at some earlier time faster than light. It is hard to believe that the highly obscure question of how such counterfactuals are to be evaluated has to be settled before one can rationally believe all F's to be G's. So suppose the relocation theorist instead cites as commitments only those conditionals whose antecedents mention places the believer could reach. Then the problem is that these commitments fail to determine the truth conditions. Their fulfilment would require all the F's at places the thinker could reach to be G; they would not require all F's whatsoever to be G. Thus take someone who believes that all the planets other than Earth (in some solar system or other) which he could encounter are uninhabited; he need not also believe that *all* planets other than Earth are uninhabited, but according to the latest version of the relocation theory he would be counted as doing so.[13] The

---

[13] As one might anticipate, these difficulties also arise for Hintikka's game-theoretic semantics for the quantifiers. These semantics include such clauses as

(G.E)   If [a formula] G is of the form ($\exists$ x)A, I choose a member of [the domain] D, give it a name, say 'n' (if it did not have one before). The game is continued with respect to A(n/x) . . . the result of substituting 'n' for 'x' in A.

(*Logic, Language-Games and Information* (Oxford: O.U.P., 1973), p. 100: I have changed the notation in unimportant ways.) Hintikka adds

Revised Account treats objects which are accessible to the thinker and those which are not as uniform in respect of their relevance to unrestricted quantification: if the inaccessible places are thought of as bearing certain spatial relation to the thinker, they will still be within the range of his quantifiers.[14]

The Revised Account was outlined for currently existing physical objects. But it is an instance of a general form which can be applied to some other ranges of object. In the case of quantification over times, for example, we would equally want to say that we conceive of this domain as closed under such operations as 'the time bearing temporal relation T to t': applied to any time already in the domain, if the operation gives any value at all, that value is also in the domain. Again, the concept of the relevant temporal relations T is indefinitely extensible. In some other domains, because of special features of the range of objects in question we do not need to appeal to indefinite extensibility in the determination of the range: we

---

All human limitations have to be abstracted from. The searcher in question will have to be thought of, if not as omnipresent, then at least 'omni-nimble', free of all those limitations of access we humans are subject to. (*Ibid.*, p. 103.)

This caveat is motivated by the desire that the semantics deliver the classically correct truth conditions for the quantified sentences. Consider the sentence 'All F's are G', and suppose that it is false, but only because some inaccessible F's are not G: all the accessible F's are G. In running through Hintikka's semantic rules, we learn that for 'All F's are G' to be true, it has to be true that there is nothing we can find or choose which is $\sim G$. (Here I am assuming the version in which Nature is not personalized, and in which universally quantified matrices are rewritten as negated existential quantification of the negation of the given matrix: see *Logic, Language-Games and Information*, p. 101.) Without the imagined property of being 'omni-nimble', that could be true, and yet the universal quantification 'All F's are G' false. Now since we are not in fact omni-nimble, as Dummett has repeatedly and convincingly insisted, any account of the quantifiers which mentions that property will have to say what features of our thought give it the same truth conditions as the thoughts and utterances of the imagined beings who do have it. (Even if Hintikka were not to accept Dummett's point, there remains an internal difficulty for his semantics. If we were omni-nimble, we could travel faster than light. But the sentence 'Everything travels no faster than light' is actually true: how can Hintikka's semantics acknowledge that it is true? We could also make the point with 'No one is omni-nimble'.)

[14] If we adopt the Revised Account, we will want to say that the sense in which we cannot find an object of a particular kind when a universal quantification is true, where this abstracts from all human limitations, is itself to be explained by appeal to the existence or nonexistence of a place with an object of the given kind located – rather than conversely. It remains, of course, a question how we can so much as have the conception of inaccessible places and times, such as those outside our present and our ancestors' light cones: I discuss this in Chapter 5 below.

know that all natural numbers, for instance, will be captured by the ancestral of the successor function applied to 0. So we can say that one who judges 'All natural numbers are G' is committed to all instances of 'If n is $sss.\,.\,.s0$, then n is G', where the number of applications of the successor functor 's' is any natural number; any other commitments of the judgement are derivative from this family of commitments.

The Revised Account allows a level of uniformity in the description of universal quantification over concrete objects and natural numbers. In particular, it does not make knowledge of what would constitute a proof of a content of the form 'All natural numbers are G' a prerequisite for grasp of such contents. In adopting the Revised Account, we take at face value the situation of someone who understands quantifiers over natural numbers, but who does not know how such contents would be proved – the situation of all of us before we discovered or learned inductive proofs. What we learn when this method of proof is taught is that certain premises guarantee the truth of a content previously grasped. Consider someone who does not know of the existence of inductive proofs: is his understanding of quantification over all natural numbers necessarily defective? We will not want to insist generally on conclusive means of establishing quantifications, since this is not to be had for *a posteriori* quantifications over concrete objects. Nor is knowledge of proof conditions required for understanding, or for establishing, complex contents in which universal quantifications are embedded. If the truth condition really is determined by the canonical commitments, a thinker who knows nothing of proof-conditions in the arithmetical case may be able to appreciate that if his commitments in judging 'All F's are G' and 'Fa' are fulfilled, so too will be the commitments he incurs in judging 'Ga'. This can establish for him the complex content 'If all F's are G and a is F, then a is G' without his knowing any proof-conditions for the universal quantification.[15]

[15] What of other quantifiers? I will discuss existential quantification in Chapter 6. What of a quantifier like 'Most F's are G'? It can be said to have as canonical grounds any pair of contents of the form 'the number of F's which are $G = m$' and 'the number of F's $= n$', where most of the numbers less than or equal to n are less than or equal to m. (Here I trample on the use/mention distinction, but avoidably.) The content 'Most F's are G' is true just in case some such pair of contents is true.

The Revised Account has no natural extension to universal quantification over the real numbers, or over large totalities of sets. There may be, then, a more general account of universal quantification which is applicable over all domains whatsoever. The Revised Account is at best partial. But we can still hope that, for the areas with which it deals, the Revised Account would be a consequence of the more general account when taken together with the special features of these areas.

We will take the Revised Account as our official, though partial, elaboration of a neo-Ramseyan account of universal quantificational contents. It fits one of the general forms which we mentioned earlier, and to which we aimed to adhere: *viz.* that the canonical commitments determine the classical truth condition, in the sense that those conditions for a given thought are all fulfilled if and only if the thought is true. In giving the neo-Ramseyan account, we have at no point made use of the idea of a human, or any idealized thinker, being able to recognize that the truth condition for a universally quantified thought obtains. Dummett has written

> since . . . from the supposition that the condition for the truth of a mathematical statement, as platonistically understood, obtains, it cannot in general be inferred that it is one which a human being need be supposed to be even capable of recognizing as obtaining, we cannot give substance to the conception of our having an implicit knowledge of what that condition is, since nothing that we do can amount to a manifestation of such knowledge.[16]

The neo-Ramseyan account suggests that the classical truth condition is manifested not by a thinker's actions when he recognizes the truth condition to obtain, but rather by his commitments when he judges the universal quantification: for all of those commitments to be fulfilled, the classical truth condition has to obtain, albeit that it is not conclusively knowable that it does so. For each one of these commitments,

---

[16] *Elements of Intuitionism* (Oxford: O.U.P., 1977), at p. 375. See also his *Frege: Philosophy of Language* (London: First Edition, Duckworth, 1973), p. 465: 'On a realistic conception of meaning, an understanding of a sentence consists in a knowledge of what has to be the case for it to be true; and such knowledge must, in turn, consist in a model for what it would be to recognize the sentence as true by the most direct means.' It is the 'must' here which I am questioning.

the thinker can manifest that it is one of his commitments: that the thinker judges a content with a particular family of commitments is not unmanifestable. Dummett regards the classical truth condition for universal quantifications as illegitimately projected from observational cases, where he holds that it is legitimate and correct to speak of a thinker's ability to recognize that the truth condition for a sentence obtains.[17] But according to the present account, the observational case itself displays the same structure as the neo-Ramseyan account of quantification. The thought 'That box is cubic' has the truth condition it does because the canonical commitments of the thinker – roughly that in suitable circumstances the box would be perceived as cubic from different angles – are fulfilled if and only if the box really does have the shape of a cube. When we reflect on the observational case, it appears that there is no need to appeal to a thinker's recognition of a truth condition as obtaining for there to be manifestation of grasp of a classical truth condition: and no possibility of so appealing either, when we reflect on the irregular quadrilaterals and the rest. On the neo-Ramseyan account, universal quantification is just another illustration of this general point. There are special features peculiar respectively to observational concepts and to quantifiers; and there are mistaken ways of defending the classical truth conditions, many of which have been criticized by Dummett; but there remains on the present theory of content a level at which, in respect of the relations between truth and manifestation, observational and universal quantificational contents are structurally identical.

The general Conjecture we formulated at the start of Chapter 2 can be made more convincing only by the detailed investigation of many other problematic kinds of content. We will consider some of them in later chapters. The model of a content p and its associated canonical grounds $G(p)$ or commitments $C(p)$ is in no way sacrosanct in carrying out this programme. It is plausible that something different will be needed where the concept in question is governed by inferential principles. It may also be that for some contents – perhaps

---

[17] See 'What is a Theory of Meaning? (II)', *op. cit.* especially p. 98ff.

contents about inaccessible places and times – we need to draw on truth conditions of contents for which we already have a plausible implementation of the programme; these would then be cases to which the second clause of our initial Conjecture would apply. But this is all speculative and tentative. So far all I have tried to do is to outline an implementation in the case of two sorts of content. As for the general programme, at the moment we can say only this: whatever difficulties may attend the treatment of other contents, there is no sound argument in advance of detailed investigation that acceptance conditions cannot determine realistic truth conditions.

PART II

GENERALIZATIONS AND EXTENSIONS

4

Individuating Content

In Chapter 1, I noted that a theory of content should contain two parts: one part should give the general form of a substantive account of content, and the other should give specifications of that general form for particular types of content. In this chapter much of my concern will be with matters of general form; in the next, I will resume consideration of particular types of content. Without some consideration of the general form of substantive accounts of content, we will not be well placed to work out substantive specifications for the myriad types of content not so far treated; nor will we be well equipped to justify the features of the proposals given in the preceding two chapters.

Those proposals made use of the idea of the canonical grounds and of the canonical commitments of a content. It is not a thesis of this essay that every content has either canonical grounds or canonical commitments: in the next chapter, I will consider contents which arguably have neither. But even in the case of contents which have canonical grounds or commitments, we ought to address the questions 'What is the general form of such a ground or commitment?' and 'What is the relation of this general form to the notion of a content we have been using?'. It will be a convenient abbreviation to speak of the *canonical links* of a content: these will be its canonical grounds, if it has such, or its canonical commitments if it has any. We can start on these general issues of form by considering the attitude of judgement.

The attitude of judgement is well-suited to occupy a central position in an account of content. This is so because truth is internal to judgement in a way in which it is not internal to many other attitudes. The point is not just that to judge p is to judge that it is true that p. For equally to hope that p is to hope that it is true that p, and to fear that p is to fear that it is true that p; but hope and fear should not occupy a central position in a theory of thought. The point is rather that truth is one of the *aims* of judgement. A thinker aims to make this the case: that he judges that p only if it is true that p.[1] Both realists and anti-realists about truth in a given area may agree on this, even if they disagree on the conditions required for us to make sense of such aiming. A thinker may try to get another person, or his own later self, to judge something which he does not at the time of his attempt take to be true; but at any given time truth is one aim of each of the judgements he makes at that time.

Judgement is not the only attitude that aims at truth. Judgement lies on a spectrum: on one side of it lies conjecture, on the other lies certainty. Both of these equally aim at truth, but they differ from judgement in their respective evidential standards. But in using judgement in an account of content, we will not be concerned with the properties which place it at a particular point on this spectrum. We will try to appeal only to those properties it has in virtue of its aiming at the truth.

On the notion of content used throughout this essay, what is required for a given content to be true is always intrinsic to that content: it is something constitutive of the content's identity. Judgement aims at truth of the content judged. So in learning what is necessarily involved in judging a given content, we can

[1] Dummett has often emphasized that sometimes more goes into the determination of the truth of a sentence than its content – notably when what he calls "ingredient sense" is more discriminating than content sense: see *Frege: Philosophy of Language* Second Edition, Index. I have not qualified the text, since it is not apparent that we can make the same distinction for contents (Thoughts) as for sentences. In particular, consider two sentences which have the same content sense but different ingredient senses: 'The F is G' and 'dthat(the F) is G' is one such pair. (For 'dthat( )', see D. Kaplan, *Demonstratives Draft #2*, UCLA mimeo, 1977.) These sentences are distinct as a matter of syntax: but there is no such thing as the analogue of purely syntactic, non-semantic, structure for thoughts in the sense used in this essay.

learn something about the nature of that particular content itself. Judgement in fact gives us a means of introducing a notion of canonical grounds and commitments. A canonical commitment of the content that p is something which, if a thinker finds it fails to hold, constitutively requires him to judge that not-p (if the question arises in thought), and to do so for the reason that it fails to hold. The commitment is indefeasible on this characterization. A canonical ground for the content that p is something which, if a thinker finds it holds, constitutively requires him (should the question arise in thought) to judge that p, and to do so for the reason that it holds.[2]

These criteria are both *attributional* and *reason-oriented*. They are attributional because if someone fails to be sensitive to the failure of canonical commitments or to the holding of canonical grounds for a content on these criteria, he cannot be attributed the ability to judge that content. They are reason-oriented because they are framed in terms of reasons for judging. We will try to sharpen these rough, intuitive criteria soon.

How is the fact that truth conditions are intrinsic to contents to be reconciled with an acceptance-condition theory of content? Is there a residue of truth conditions unexplained by factors relating to acceptance? If that were so then content would not have been fully explained in terms of acceptance conditions. There would also be the problem of explaining how the features of a content relating to acceptance and the features determining its truth value are related. No such problems arise, though, if the acceptance conditions of a content ultimately themselves determine its truth condition. That is the Conjecture for which I argued in the preceding chapters for two particular kinds of content, and I will discuss it again later. If a theorist

---

[2] These definitions by themselves cannot settle the question of whether there are also important constitutive *prima facie* or defeasible notions which should be used in a substantive account of particular contents. But it is worth noting that some constitutive and *prima facie* relations are consequential upon the specification of indefeasible grounds or commitments. For example, a subject has a *prima facie* but inconclusive reason for judging a content when a wide range of the canonical commitments of a content have been found true and none falsified. It is a question worthy of further consideration whether all *prima facie* grounds of a relatively *a priori* kind can be explained by their relations to indefeasible commitments or grounds.

maintains that content of the kind we are considering is determined by certain acceptance conditions, and he also wants to offer a unitary notion of content, then he must defend such a thesis of determination of truth conditions by acceptance conditions.

The schematic form of a canonical commitment of a particular content can, to a first approximation, be given thus. If the content is not to be rejected, then if (i) certain contents are true and (ii) the thinker is in certain mental states, then (iii) certain other contents will be true and (iv) the thinker will be in certain other mental states. So a canonical commitment can be represented by a 4-tuple of sets, corresponding to (i)–(iv). The first and third components will be sets of contents, while the second and fourth will be sets of mental states. Any one of these sets may be empty.

This is all concerned with what a canonical commitment *is*. When we come to the question of what it is for a thinker to manifest that a 4-tuple is a commitment of a given thought, we have to be concerned not with the truth of contents in the 4-tuple, but with their acceptance; and we have to be concerned not with a mental state, but with whether the thinker is in it. On a particular occasion, one way a thinker may manifest that a 4-tuple $\langle$(i), (ii), (iii), (iv)$\rangle$ is a commitment of a given thought that p is as follows. Suppose he accepts all the contents in (i) and is in all the mental states in (ii); then if either there is some content in (iii) he does not accept, or there is some mental state in (iv) he is not in, he will judge that not-p if the question arises. We should add that his reason for doing so will be these facts about (i)–(iv).

It would be a mistake to think that components (i) and (iii) of the 4-tuple – the sets of contents – can be absorbed by the second and fourth, by including there additionally the mental states of belief in those contents. To do so would likely be based on a failure to distinguish what a commitment *is* from what is involved in a thinker's manifesting that it is a commitment of one of the thoughts in his repertoire. As we noted, acceptance and so belief are indeed involved in the latter. But to have *only* mental states in the specification of the former – of what the commitment *is* – could be correct only for contents about the thinker's own mental states: it could not be correct for contents about the world around him. It is true that in the account in Chapter 2 perceptual experience was mentioned in the canonical commitments of observational contents. It was in the commitments of observational thoughts that perceptual experience was mentioned: and in those cases I argued that the whole family of commitments of a given thought entails an environmental condition. It is only because this is so that that account was not a non-starter.

Four-tuples of the sort just considered can also serve to capture canonical grounds. Suppose of one such four-tuple that it is in the canonical grounds of a given content that p. The idea would then be this. Suppose a thinker accepts the contents of the first and is in the mental states of the second component of the given 4-tuple. If he also accepts the contents in the third component and is in the mental states of the fourth, he is rationally required to judge the content that p, should the question arise in thought. In any formal development of such a theory, there would have to be some labelling to distinguish the case in which a four-tuple is specifying a ground and that in which it is specifying a commitment.

This account allows that the canonical links of a given content may consist of various *sets* of mental states and contents. So it is possible that the canonical commitments of a given thought take the form that the subject's states and the contents which are true are those which would be expected if a certain kind of theory were true: it may be constitutive of possession of the concepts in the given thought that they be applied in accordance with the constraints of a more or less schematic theory. That this is so would not be a matter of dispute for application of the concepts of belief and desire, or for the ability to make judgements about how things are at places other than one's current location. The canonical links of a particular thought may be given by some single type of content or experience: but if such theoretical structures are what unify the various 4-tuples in the canonical links, they do not have to be given so simply.

In an investigation at a more detailed level than that at which I am currently proceeding, one would have to consider whether this representation of canonical links is not unduly restrictive. For instance, some thoughts have an essential connection with action: for there are action-based ways of thinking of things. A particular type of gesture, which a subject is able to make on demand, even when the limb with which he makes it is anaesthetized, may be thought of by the agent in such a way; when thought of in such a way, it may come as a surprise to him to see precisely what shape his limb traces when he makes the gesture thought of that way. Equally a pianist is capable of thinking of a chord in an action-based way, one whose employment is compatible with his not knowing which notes compose it or even, without further reflection, exactly which fingers he is pressing on the keyboard when he sounds it. What seems to be constitutive of these modes of presentation is that when a thinker acts on an intention to perform an action thought of in one of these ways, he tries to act in a certain way (and does so in favourable circumstances). We cannot make sense of the possibility that someone is employing just these ways of thinking of a movement in the content of his intentions without such connections obtaining. The very idea of canonical links has been explained in terms of judgement. But these points might tempt someone into saying that thoughts containing these ways of thinking have to be explained by their connections not with judgement, but with intention. Such a conclusion would be premature. There is no reason that the canonical links of a thought should not mention the outcome of performing certain types of action. Its canonical commitments, for instance, may mention the outcome of actions performed in executing intentions whose contents contain the distinctive action-based ways of thinking. That such mention has to be made may be just what is distinctive of such thoughts. The essential connection with intention is preserved, because a thinker must be capable of certain types of action if he is to be capable of displaying sensitivity to such canonical links. These action-based thoughts are intriguing, but not central to our present concerns. I will not be further concerned with them here.

A specification of the canonical links of a given content is intended to be *a priori*, rather than an empirical, descriptive theory. *A fortiori*, then, it is not a descriptive theory of the subpersonal confirmation behaviour of sentences in a subpersonal language of thought. The norms it outlines are norms for persons to follow. If we talk of subpersonal systems making judgements for reasons – which may be heuristically valuable – that is a *façon de parler*. The talk of reasons in a specification of canonical links is by contrast to be taken literally.

It may be helpful to distinguish the several points at which normative considerations, broadly having to do with rationality or reasons, may be introduced in this area. (i) They may be brought into an account of content, so that the account of what it is to grasp a content makes reference to what would give reasons for or against judging that content. This is probably the least controversial point at which to introduce them. (ii) They may enter an account of truth itself: an example would be Putnam's view that truth is no more than rational acceptability under sufficiently good epistemic conditions.[3] (iii) They may be introduced into a theory of knowledge which makes epistemic status sometimes turn on normative aspects of content and their relations to the believer. I am in the middle of arguing for (i) and will be making a case for (iii) in Chapter 10. Anyone who holds (i) will suppose that normativeness is in some way connected with truth, since truth conditions are intrinsic to content: but it does not follow that, for example, one has to accept Putnam's thesis about truth. It is also a separate question from (i)–(iii) whether rationality can be given an illuminating reductive analysis.

There are several virtues which we should require of a statement of the canonical links which individuate a particular content. We ought to require uniqueness and completeness. To say that a statement of the canonical links for a given content is uniquely determining (for brevity, *unique*) is to say that the content is the only one which has the constitutive grounds or commitments stated. To say that such a statement is *complete* is to say that it includes explicitly or implicitly every aspect of the thought's canonical links. For contents which are individuated by their canonical links, completeness implies uniqueness. If it did not, there could be two such contents with the same pattern of canonical links; so one would have to conclude that their

[3] H. Putnam, *Philosophical Papers, Volume 3: Realism and Reason* (Cambridge: C.U.P., 1983), p. 231.

canonical links do not exhaust what determines the identity of such a content. So, to give a maximally simple example, the natural deduction rules which are common to classical alternation and to exclusive disjunction are not *all* of the rules for both connectives; and when we do add the rest of the rules which separate them and obtain completeness for each one, we also obtain uniqueness of both accounts. We will also want a compositionality requirement: an account of the canonical links of a given content should be exhibitable as a resultant of the contributions made by that content's various constituents. Each constituent will make a uniform contribution to the canonical links of the contents in which it occurs: this contribution must be specified and from it, the correct pattern of canonical links for contents containing the constituent must be shown to result.

A theorist might attempt, for some fundamental level of contents, to specify canonical grounds and commitments of which a thinker can tell infallibly whether they hold or not. This theorist can be said to be following an *inward-looking method*. His canonical grounds and commitments must not concern perception, knowledge and memory, since the subject can be mistaken about whether he is in those states. The inward-looking theorist's canonical grounds and commitments will rather concern the subject's experiences, conscious beliefs and apparent memories.[4] The inward-looking theorist can allow inductive uncertainty about the fulfilment of the grounds and commitments he builds up from such components: but the inductive uncertainty will for him always concern ultimately some condition of which the thinker will in the appropriate circumstances be in a position to tell infallibly whether it holds or not. The appropriate circumstances may, for instance, be a matter of waiting for a certain time to come round.

The inward-looking theorist seems to be faced with insoluble problems. If someone's experiences and apparent memories

---

[4] This is not to say that what gives a conscious state its content is independent of its relations to the external world. On the contrary, what makes an experience represent something as spherical, for example, must ultimately be a matter of its relations to instances in the world of the property of being spherical. But this is consistent with a subject's lacking infallible knowledge of whether an experience of something as spherical on a particular occasion is a hallucination.

and beliefs are being produced by Descartes' evil demon, or if he is a brain in a vat, all the infallibly establishable grounds and commitments for some perceptual judgement the subject attempts to make may be fulfilled and all his inductive expectations met: yet since he is perceiving nothing, his attempts at perceptual judgements do not result in anything true, while those of a perceiving subject in the same inner conditions may be true. This implies that the inward-looking theorist must be omitting something relevant to content, on the Fregean conception thereof: for here there is difference of truth value without any difference in fulfilment of the canonical links of the sort he cites as determining content. One might be tempted to say that the inward-looking theorist is achieving only an account of the content 'It is from the inside as if it were the case that p', rather than the content that p itself. But even this would be too strong: for the content 'It is from the inside as if it were the case that p' embeds the content that p, and the inward-looking theorist does not have an account even of this unless he has an account of the embedded content that p. The inward-looking theorist might propose simply to add to the canonical links for some of his contents a presupposed condition, that the subject is perceiving (or remembering &c.). But the content of this presupposition would not then have been explained in conformity with the principles the inward-looking theorist followed in the case of his other conditions: in fact he would not have explained its content at all.[5]

This argument still stands even if it is insisted that the presupposed condition that the subject is perceiving need not be one that he himself can think: perhaps only we, as theorists, need to be able to formulate it. Still, it is a condition we theorists are capable of thinking: and so there is still a content the inward-looking theorist has not explained.

For rather primitive contents and concepts, an outward-

[5] The argument of this paragraph would not get a grip against a theorist who says that a content's acceptance conditions do not determine its truth conditions. Does the vat subject at least show that such a theorist may have an inward-looking theory of *his* favoured acceptance conditions? I will be arguing that the only contents used in thought at the personal level which do characterize the vat subject's mental states are ones whose nature has to be explained by the outward-looking model below, and not the inward-looking model. *If* that is so, not even such a theorist can use the inward-looking model.

looking method is more promising. Outward-looking methods aim to detail the relations to external objects and their properties which a subject must have in order to be capable of having attitudes to certain contents about those objects and properties. Such a method was followed in Chapter 2, when we said that the canonical commitments of a thought that a perceptually presented object is cubic is that in specified counterfactual circumstances the object be *perceived* as thus-and-so. This is just one amongst many conceivable outward-looking accounts. The problem that faced the inward-looking theorist will then not arise for an outward-looking theorist at all: the subject who is on a particular occasion deceived by the evil demon or the scientist manipulating the brain placed in the vat does not stand in the relations to external objects required by any plausible outward-looking account if he is to succeed in referring to an external material object when he attempts to think 'That cat is black'.[6] It will then not surprise the outward-looking theorist that so many of a subject's judgements are not true.

Correlatively, an outward-looking theorist is likely to find one form of radical scepticism intelligible, whether or not it is refutable. This will be the form of scepticism concerned with the possibility that on a particular occasion it is for a thinker subjectively as if he stands in the appropriate relations to external objects to be capable of referring to them in thought, but does not in fact do so.[7] This is one of many points at which epistemology and a substantive theory of content are inextricable.[8]

The inward-looking theorist, and others, may press the question 'How can a thinker's judgements or actions possibly manifest the features of content attributed in an outward-

[6] The cagey phrase 'attempts to think . . .' is to highlight the fact that the present general point is independent of one's stance on the issue of whether a genuine perceptual-demonstrative content can be thought by a totally hallucinating subject.

[7] For the outward-looking theorist, the role of perception in his account will be reflected (though of course not exhausted) in the conditions under which a thinker will withdraw an attempted perceptual judgement, since those conditions will include evidence of hallucination.

[8] Scepticism is beyond the scope of this essay: though of course no theory of content should be endorsed before its consequences for scepticism have been traced out. I return to other epistemological issues in Chapters 9 and 10.

looking account? In the nature of the case, must these not go beyond what can, up to inductive uncertainty, be infallibly confirmed?' But this question can be answered. Call a content *internal* for a thinker iff it is not possible, in conditions which are ideal relative to that thinker and that content, that the content be rationally acceptable for him and yet be false. How can a thinker manifest his grasp of contents which are not internal for him? In the nature of the case, not by his responses to infallibly knowable conditions. But his grasp of contents which are not internal can still be manifested in part by conditions concerning his relations to his environment which themselves are not internal. He will (roughly) withdraw his earlier judgement 'That box is cubic' made of a perceptually presented box in front of him if he keeps track of it and from a different angle has a perception of it as some other shape: and many other similar conditionals relating him to the perceived object will hold. A second thinker can in turn know that these conditionals are true of the first, if he himself is suitably related to the environment and sensitive to the first subject's relations to it: again in knowing this he will be knowing a content which is not internal for him. There is no question here of an unmanifestability of the distinctive objective reference in the content acknowledged by the outward-looking theorist. Relations between a thinker and his environment may not exhaust what has to be mentioned in an account of grasp of a given content: in Chapter 2 we suggested that the thinker may also need some conception of these relations. But mention of such relations is still an essential component of such an account.

The inward-looking theorist is in a particularly weak position in putting this manifestation challenge: for he does not have a reduced content to offer. We argued that 'It is as if it were the case that *p*' is unavailable to him. A more direct description of sequences of experiences would also be unavailable if these two plausible conditions hold: (a) experiences of a given type have to be thought of as states which stand in various complex relations to objective, perceivable states of affairs, and (b) the ability to have thoughts about such states of affairs requires the capacity on occasion to make perceptual-demonstrative judgements 'That is an *F*', where the demonstrative refers to an external material object. For this last type of thought was precisely what seemed unavailable to the inward-looking theorist.

There is a distinction between two very different kinds of canonical link: it is a distinction which cuts across that between grounds and commitments. Consider the content that some given person believes a certain conditional 'If p were to be the case, then q would also be the case'. It is, roughly, a canonical ground of this that the person in question *intends* to bring it about that q by bringing it about that p. (Necessary refinements do not affect the point I am about to make.) A thought which is not treated as established by the given person's intention is not the thought that the person believes the counterfactual. Here the canonical ground embeds the concept of intention. But we should not conclude from this that intention is in some way conceptually more fundamental than belief, that it could be understood without any grasp of belief. For the notion of canonical grounds and commitments we have characterized is consistent with the concepts used in the specification of the canonical links being of the same level of sophistication as those in the content for which they are canonical links. In some cases the canonical links *are* of a kind which can be grasped without grasping the contents for which they are canonical links. The canonical ground p for a content p *or* q would be an example, and so would some of the quantificational cases of Chapter 3. But it is not so for all canonical links.

Again, it will be useful to label the distinction. We will say that a thought has *lower-level* canonical links if someone could have all the concepts from which the contents in its canonical links are composed, without having all the concepts of the given thought. A ground or commitment was represented by a 4-tuple comprised of a set of contents, a set of mental states, another set of contents, and another set of mental states. The phrase 'contents in the canonical links' in the characterization of lower-level links is here intended to cover not just the contents in the first and third components of the 4-tuple. It is also intended to include the contents of the mental states in the second and fourth components. It would include, for instance, the propositional representational content of a perceptual experience. The contents in the canonical links in any of these senses we will sometimes call the 'content ingredients' of the canonical links. A thought has *same-level* canonical links if it does not have lower-level canonical links. The immediate question the distinction between same-level and lower-level links raises is whether the canonical links which individuate content must be lower-level. The claim that they must be is a relatively strong form of reductionism.

I will be arguing against the reductionist claim that content-individuating canonical links have to be lower-level. Nor is it only in the fundamental case that canonical links may be same-level. Local holisms may occur at various points in a hierarchy of levels of content: in fact their presence seems to be the rule rather than the exception. The defining feature of their presence is that there is a family of concepts with this property: thoughts containing each concept have same-level canonical links whose content ingredients contain other concepts from the family.

If content had always to be explained in terms of lower-level canonical links, then there would be an infinite regress. Though there are infinitely many contents, for a given thinker, there will be only finitely many primitive constituents of these thoughts. Canonical links will be specified for each type containing one of these primitive constituents: there will be only finitely many content-determining specifications.[9] The threat of regress means that we must either abandon the view that canonical links have to be lower-level, or else we must give up the view that in cases where there are no lower-level links, content is determined by canonical links.

It might be suggested that the regress objection could be blocked by saying that if the canonical links for a content are given by the holding of other contents *tout court*, then they must be of lower level, but if the canonical links are given, say, in terms of perceptual experience, they need not be of lower level. The hope behind this move would then be that at the most fundamental level, that is of contents concerning the

---

[9] When there are demonstrative constituents, the content-determining specifications will be given for all demonstratives of a given primitive type (*e.g.* all present-tense constituents): so again there will be only finitely many.

observational properties of perceived things in the thinker's environment, there could be same-level canonical links concerning perceptual experience: so the regress would be blocked. But the move seems to involve inconsistent standards. The concepts which feature in the content of judgements at the fundamental level – concepts of things being particular colours, of certain three-dimensional shapes, of particular familiar kinds – are concepts which feature in the representational content of perceptual experiences too. It is not in general true that some of the concepts in the content of a fundamental judgement will not feature in the content of the perceptual experiences mentioned in giving the judged content's canonical links. So it will *not* be true that someone could, without having all the concepts in one of these fundamental contents, have all the concepts used in the content ingredients of its canonical links. What could be the rationale for accepting a lower-level requirement for the first and third components of a canonical link, while rejecting it for the second and fourth?

The local holism of the fundamental level is in fact quite extensive. How would we confirm that the canonical commitments of a thought of a perceptually presented object 'That lump is cubic' are fulfilled? Doing so involves testing an array of simple but still non-observational assumptions, which have somehow to be borne out by experience. *(a)* The thinker has to be able to confirm that he has changed location and in such a way that he is enjoying a different perspective on the same object. This has to be confirmed in part by his changing experience of *other* objects as his spatial relations to them vary. How these experiences will change depends upon the shapes of those objects in turn: the thought that such an object has a certain shape is a thought of the same kind as the original thought whose confirmation is in question. This suggests, unsurprisingly, that one can only confirm several such propositions simultaneously. *(b)* In *(a)* it is already presumed that one can check how a thing would have looked earlier from a particular angle by later moving to that angle. This involves some hypothesis about the stability of shape over time, and again some simple use of a criterion of identity over time. *(c)* Further, in the general case these evidential procedures are reliable only if the shape of the given lump of matter is not influenced by the subject's changing location; a thinker whose judgements were not sensitive to his exposure to evidence that there is such a dependence would not be employing the same content as occurs in our judgement 'that lump is cubic'. I have been describing "confirmation" of the non-observational assumptions *(a) – (c)* in a way more appropriate to a reflective theorist than to a non-philosophical perceiver. What really matters is that the unreflective perceiver should, in his simple perceptual and spatial judgements, be sensitive to the same bodies of evidence in the same way as might a reflective theorist who does consciously test these assumptions. Beneath all the interlocking simple judgements which *are* made by the unreflective perceiver, there is of course an underlying level of nonrational sensori-motor and memory skills, on whose existence use of this fundamental level of content rests.

We earlier slipped into talking of a hierarchy of contents without defining it. One type of thought is *immediately above* another if all thoughts of the first type have lower-level canonical links whose content ingredients include some thoughts of the second type. The relation of being *above* is the ancestral of the relation of being immediately above. (Nothing in this definition excludes the possibility that, of two distinct types of thought, neither is above the other.) For a type of thought which has canonical links, we can speak of its place in a *Grand Partial Ordering* of types. We will also need some notions of aboveness for concepts. We can say that one concept is *above* another if *(a)* for any thought containing the first concept which has canonical links at all, some of its content ingredients contain the second concept, and *(b)* someone could possess the second concept without possessing the first. It seems, for example, plausible that the concept of a person's having an experience as of something red in front of him is above the concept of a physical object's *being* red; and thoughts containing the concept of an experience of red are above those containing the concept of a red object.[10]

[10] These points are argued in my 'Consciousness and Other Minds', *Proceedings of the Aristotelian Society Supplementary Volume* **58** (1984), pp. 97–117. In giving this example of the *above* relation, I am not saying that the commitments of a thought about experiences of red which contain the concept of being red *exhaust* its content: only that they should not be omitted. For an outline of a hierarchical conception of content, formulated at the linguistic level in terms of understanding, see Dummett's

Contents which have the same canonical links we will call *evidentially equivalent*. Now it seems that there are evidentially equivalent contents which are nevertheless distinct. Consider the familiar pair 'There is a rabbit nearby' and 'There is an undetached rabbit part nearby', or the pair 'There was a rabbit here yesterday' and 'There was a rabbit-stage here yesterday'. Canonical grounds and canonical commitments have so far been specified simply as sets of a certain type of 4-tuple. For each of these pairs of contents, it seems that anything which might be a canonical ground for one would equally be a canonical ground for the other; and conversely; and similarly for canonical commitments. So the members of each pair are evidentially equivalent but distinct. How are these examples to be reconciled with the thesis that their canonical links individuate the contents that have such links? If the constituent concepts 'rabbit' and 'undetached rabbit part' had already been established to be distinct on the present substantive conception, we could argue by appeal to structure that the contents are distinct: but we have not yet established that antecedent.

Do these pairs of contents mean that we have to look to something quite different from the canonical links thoughts in order to give an account of their identity? No: what we need to consider are the canonical links of a *range* of thoughts in which a given concept features. The two thoughts 'This rabbit is wholly black' and 'This undetached rabbit part is wholly black' do not have the same canonical links. It is because there are other thoughts, differing only in that one has the concept 'rabbit' where the other has the concept 'undetached rabbit part', and which have different canonical links, that the thoughts 'There is a rabbit nearby' and 'There is an undetached

---

important paper 'The Justification of Deduction' (repr. in his *Truth and Other Enigmas op. cit.*). The stimulus I have received from this seminal work will be evident. But those who know that work well will note major points of divergence in the formulations above and to follow. They concern the accommodation of local holisms, the presence of formulations which leave it open how extensive they are and a different outline of the relations between truth and evidence. The link much further below with epistemology, though additional to his formulations, is certainly consistent with Dummett's general characterization. As will be clear from Chapter 8 below, the fact that Dummett's formulation is in linguistic terms is no accident: so there is also divergence over the relative priority of thought and language.

rabbit part nearby' are distinct, even though *their* canonical links are the same.

It seems, then, sufficient for the nonidentity of concepts φ and ψ that there be some concept (or more generally mode of presentation) C such that the thoughts that C(φ) and C(ψ) are not evidentially equivalent. But how are we to turn this point into a criterion? If we simply generalize it, we will be saying that concept φ and concept ψ are the same iff for any mode of presentation C with which φ and ψ may combine, the canonical links of the thought that C(φ) are the same as the canonical links of the thought C(ψ). But this formulation takes for granted the individuation of the mode of presentation C. If C were lower than φ and ψ in the grand ordering, this need not be problematic; but there is no reason to suppose that in general it would be lower. A new level of thought may introduce a new family of concepts simultaneously; and of course at the basic level for which canonical evidence is not given solely in terms of the truth of other contents, but in terms of perception and other information-giving states, C is inevitably not lower than φ and ψ.

The conclusion to be drawn from this is not that the task is impossible, but rather that we have to define the identity of a whole set of concepts of a given level simultaneously, without taking for granted the individuation of any concepts of that level. Within such an approach we can still aim to capture the idea that concepts or modes of presentation are the same if, however combined, the resulting thoughts have the same canonical evidence at the lower level. Let us try to make this sharper.

We will consider just monadic concepts and modes of presentation of objects. (The approach can easily be generalized to cover other operators.) Take the concepts $\varphi_1, \ldots, \varphi_k$, and the modes of presentation of objects $m_1, \ldots, m_n$. As before, '^' denotes the operation on thought-constituents which is the analogue of concatenation for expressions. Then I suggest that a one-one mapping correlating each concept φ_i with some concept ψ_i and each mode of presentation m_j with some mode of presentation n_j is the identity mapping if for all φ_i and all m_j the thoughts $\varphi_i \,\hat{}\, m_j$ and $\psi_i \,\hat{}\, n_j$ have the same canonical links. But what range of concepts do we have to consider? We must not make the range too small, or else we may identify distinct but evidentially equivalent thoughts; and we must not make it too large, or else impredicativity problems will arise. The appropriate range seems to be this: we must consider all concepts in the repertoire of the thinker in question which are *not above any* of the concepts in the domain or range of the one-one mapping, in the sense of aboveness we recently considered. This criterion then endorses the idea that difference of concepts depends upon difference of canonical links of some thoughts or other.

When the concern is with radical interpretation, this criterion for a mapping to be an identity mapping has to be employed in combination with other constraints upon the ascription of content. In particular it would have to be used together with the Tightness Constraint given in *Sense and Content*.[11] If there is no thought of which the subject is capable and whose canonical links distinguish between the concept "rabbit" and "undetached rabbit part", then it would be quite unempirical to attribute one concept rather than the other: some way must be provided to attribute only what is common to both.

The upshot seems to be that an acceptance-condition theorist of content, when appealing to canonical grounds and commitments, may discriminate contents at two different levels of fineness.[12] Rough-hewn contents are individuated by sameness of canonical grounds and commitments, conceived of just as sets of our 4-tuples; while fine-grained contents are individuated by sameness of constituents and modes of combination, where the identity of the constituents is constrained in the way just discussed. The fine-grained discrimination does not depend upon notions which go beyond the legitimate resources of the normative acceptance-condition theorist.

A theory of content which appeals to canonical links, and more generally acceptance-condition theories of content, can help to resolve a problem for any Fregean account of thoughts.

[11] *op. cit.* pp. 78–86.

[12] For a *very* rough parallel, compare the several levels at which the possible worlds theorist may proceed in individuating propositions: cp. D. Lewis, 'General Semantics', repr. in his *Philosophical Papers Volume 1* (Oxford: O.U.P., 1983), pp. 200–201.

The problem concerns the relative priority of thoughts and the constituents from which they are built up. Each content is conceived of as structured. This structure corresponds to what Dummett calls the analysis, as opposed to a decomposition, of the thought: it is the structure which in some way or other is necessarily grasped when the thought is grasped.[13] The problem is that we seem to have no conception of what these constituents, the modes of presentation, are apart from their role as constituents of thoughts. It is true that there are mental states whose object is not a complete propositional content, but rather a component thereof: recognizing and seeking would be examples. But we can make sense of these because of systematic connections of those states with states which do have complete thoughts as their objects. The analogies for the distinction between analysis and decomposition do not help us on this particular problem. One such analogy is the difference between the relation holding of a molecule and its constituent atoms, and the relation between a country and one of its divisions into regions: analysis is like the former, decomposition the latter. We *can* conceive of an atom existing independently of its being a constituent of a molecule; and the idea of its existing does not seem to need explanation in terms of its potential role as a molecular constituent.

I suggest that on the account I am outlining, we can consistently hold that thoughts are structured entities while simultaneously acknowledging that the nature of a mode of presentation is to be given by its role as a possible thought-constituent. On the present acceptance-condition theory, for a

---

[13] See *The Interpretation of Frege's Philosophy op. cit.* pp. 261ff. I am not suggesting that the reasons given in the present text were tacitly Frege's when he espoused the doctrine which Dummett summarizes on his p. 261: '. . . the constituents of a thought are arrived at by analysis of it'. The lack of any extensive discussion by Frege of what it is to be capable of grasping a thought precludes constrained speculation here. But I do suggest that this is a point at which a coherent defence of a Fregean theory must draw upon a substantive theory of content. I hope it is clear that the views defended in the text do *not* entail that, as Sluga would say, thoughts are grasped as wholes (cp. Dummett, *op. cit.*, pp. 294ff.). On the present theory, the analysis of a thought is a matter of features of its acceptance conditions – more particularly, for the thoughts so far considered, it is a matter of features of its canonical grounds and consequences. What makes it the case that a thinker is judging one thought rather than another is an appropriate sensitivity to these canonical links. There is, *a priori*, simply no room for grasping the thought and not grasping its structure.

thought to *have* a certain constituent just *is* for it to stand in certain relations to other thoughts and mental states: for thoughts with canonical links, the relations are those given in the canonical grounds and commitments for thoughts of the type containing that constituent. Now these relations have two features. First, they are intrinsic to the thought: they contribute to its individuation. Second, as patterns of canonical grounds and commitments, they are relations in which only a thought *can* stand. This gives a sense to, and vindicates, the view that a constituent of a thought cannot be conceived of except ultimately by its relations to thoughts. But as long as we have the Grand Partial Ordering, and adequate descriptions of the patterns of canonical links, there is no circularity in saying that the thoughts are composed of such modes of presentation. The talk of composition is just a vivid way of encoding more or less complex intrinsic features of the patterns of canonical grounds and commitments which ultimately individuate the thought.

The point should not be overstated, for it does not concern a virtue unique to an acceptance-condition account of content. Some similar solution of the problem will be available to any substantive theory of content meeting two conditions: the theory has some version of the Grand Partial Ordering of contents and it can specify which of the substantive, in-dividuating properties of a thought make it right to say that it has one structural constituent rather than another.

5

Thinking About The Inaccessible

Can the account of the relations between truth and acceptance conditions we have been developing be applied to thoughts about inaccessible places and times? In the temporal case, I shall be concerned in this chapter only with past tense thoughts which make reference to some particular past time or particular past events. So the operator 'in the past' will not itself be in the scope of this discussion, since it tacitly involves existential quantification over past times. That operator must be treated by applying whatever theory of existential contents is favoured to the domain of past times. But the discussion will include within its scope not just thoughts like 'Yesterday was sunny' and 'That battle preceded the declaration of war', but also '10,000,000,000 million years ago spherical bodies of matter existed'. So times which were experienced, times which were unexperienced and times which are arguably unexperiencable by us are within our brief; and similarly for places. Our task is to show how thoughts about particular times and places, accessible or not, conform to our initial Conjecture.

The prospects for applying the model of canonical commitments or canonical grounds to these cases are not bright. How would we do it? There is no type of pure present tense content such that some content of that type must be true whenever a past tense content is true: yet there would have to be some such type if it is to be true of a content with canonical grounds that it is true just in case one of those grounds obtains.[1] So we could not rightly assign canonical grounds to the past tense content if the canonical grounds were to be present tense contents. The same goes *pari passu* for canonical commitments. Should we look then to past tense commitments? We can certainly truly say, for instance, that a thought '200 years ago, there was a tree here' is true just in case 200 years ago, the canonical commitments of 'There is a tree here' were fulfilled. We will want the equivalence of these contents to be a consequence of a good account of mastery of temporal concepts. But such an equivalence does not itself seem to explain that mastery.[2] To give one reason why it does not: when we applied the commitment model to observational contents earlier, we could say how those commitments were manifestable in the thought and action of someone judging such a content. The content was withdrawn if the object did not appear as it should from different relative positions. But there is no question of a thinker now varying his relations to a time 200 years ago and adjusting his judgements accordingly. We have to ask: what is it about a thinker *now* that gives one of his thoughts a truth condition concerning 200 years ago?

These points are not a proof that the model of canonical grounds or commitments cannot be developed for past tense contents, but they do make it reasonable to try another approach. The Conjecture we formulated early in this essay envisaged the possibility that in some cases, the truth conditions of contents are determined by their relations to other contents whose truth conditions are already determined: this was covered by the second clause of the Conjecture. I will be developing an approach which treats contents about inaccessible places and times as falling under this second clause. An account developed in this way will have to fall into two parts. A first part will say how the truth conditions of certain contents are determined. The second part will say how

---

[1] See p. 29.

[2] In effect this suggestion imports the truth-value links into a statement of canonical commitments; it brings with it analogues of the standard objections to the view that mention of these links is enough by itself to explain mastery of the concepts they concern. See the last section of this chapter.

the truth conditions of contents about inaccessible times and places are determined by their relations to those first contents.

In the first part of the account, we will be giving an outward-looking model of certain contents, in the sense of Chapter 4. In some cases, we can even speak literally of the perception of temporal relations. This should be less controversial than it may sound. You hear a collision and then see the traffic light change; on this basis, you judge the past-tense content 'That collision occurred just before the light changed'. Here it is correct to talk of an impression of precedence, the impression that the collision preceded the changing of the light. This type of impression shares the feature of sense experience that it need not be destroyed when it is overruled by judgement. If you learn that there was a time-delay device inserted in your optic nerve on that occasion, you will withdraw the judgement of precedence, but the impression may remain. When the mechanisms are functioning properly, the impression is causally explained in part by what it is an impression of: the fact that the collision occurred before the light changed is part of the causal explanation of your impression that it did. The logical form of these attributions of impressions is at least this: x has at t the impression that: that F occurred before that G (or that: that F is moving; or that: it is accelerating). The time at which the impression occurs has to be distinguished from the temporal conceptual content of the impression; provided we do so, we will not need to be drawn into saying that the impression itself stretches back into the past.[3]

In many cases, where there is no such impression or any memory image, what is remembered will not persist when overturned by further judgement. If you apparently remember that you have been vaccinated for smallpox, but do not remember the occasion (do not remember *being* vaccinated) no impression will persist when it is demonstrated to you that you could not have been. But the reason for this is that in many

---

[3] These points on logical form should answer the worries expressed by B.A. Farrell in 'Temporal Precedence', *Proceedings of the Aristotelian Society* **73** (1972/3), at pp. 194–6. Note that, for instance, the object referred to by 'that G' in the description of the impression does not have to exist at t for x to have the impression, nor for its content to be correct.

cases, all that memory delivers is a disposition to judge a particular content: and that disposition cannot rationally persist when an obviously incompatible content comes to be judged. It can remain the case that when the mechanism is functioning properly, the disposition to judge a content is an effect of that content's truth.[4]

In applying the outward-looking model to our grasp of temporal relations and the past, we will be accepting a theory on which perception of temporal relations is essential to grasp of those relations in the following sense: such perceptions are mentioned in a constitutive account of what it is to have those temporal concepts. But in adopting such a theory, we will be rejecting a theory on which the perceptual impressions are more intimately related to possession of the temporal concepts. This is an extreme empiricist theory on which temporal concepts are supposed to be extracted from the experiences themselves. One natural reading of William James on the perception of time takes him as propounding this more extreme view:

> What is the *original* of our experience of pastness, from whence we get the meaning of the term? . . . We shall see that we have a constant feeling *sui generis* of pastness, to which every one of our experiences in turn falls a prey. To think a thing as past is to think it amongst the objects or in the direction of the objects which at the present moment appear affected by this quality. This is the original of our notion of past time, upon which memory and history build their systems.[5]

To speak as we did of "extraction" is metaphorical, and it is a delicate matter to give a more explicit formulation of the extreme empiricist view. It can hardly be described as the view

---

[4] These impressions of precedence are counterexamples to the claim that any judgement-independent deliverances of a perceptual mechanism are experiences in a specific sense modality. The impression that the (auditorily presented) collision preceded the (visually presented) change of the lights is not itself in any sense modality.

[5] *The Principles of Psychology, Vol. I,* Ch. 15; p. 570 in the revised edition of Harvard University Press (Cambridge, Mass.), 1981. Many of James's statements on time bear more than one reading, since he never distinguishes the extreme empiricist view from the outward-looking view which will be defended here. But his continual emphasis on the nature of the subjective experience itself, and the absence of further components in his description of mastery of temporal concepts strongly favours the extreme empiricist reading.

that once a subject has impressions as of one event following another, he has the concept of temporal precedence. That is a formulation of the relatively uncontentious point that it is the concept of temporal precedence itself, and nothing weaker, which enters the content of the impression of succession and motion; and this uncontentious point is neutral on the nature of possession of temporal concepts. It is equally neutral on these issues to say: an event is past just in case it stands to some present event in the ancestral of the relation in which two events are experienced as standing when one is experienced as preceding the other. That is true: but it is not a theory of what it is to have the concept of the past.

We need a better formulation of extreme empiricism. There may be various forms of extreme empiricism, but one component of a description of mastery of the concept of temporal precedence seems implicit in all of them. This is the component stating that if a thinker with such mastery has the impression that one event preceded another, and the question arises in thought of whether the one did precede the other, he ought rationally to judge that it did. The forms of extreme empiricism differ in the accounts developed for judgements not based on such impressions.

Thus characterized, extreme empiricism faces a dilemma. Is it conceivable or not that an experience of precedence (for instance) should be non-veridical? If it is not, it is hardly our familiar notion of experience which is being used. Temporal impressions, like any other deliverance of a perceptual mechanism, are subject to hallucination. This is true both in respect of ordering and in respect of magnitude: in some actual cases, a person may complete a sentence the first words of which he uttered weeks ago, and have the impression on completion that he has just uttered the whole sentence.[6] If the extreme empiricist agrees that these experiences need not be veridical, then he owes us an account of how this can be so: that is, a statement of what it is about a subject's use of temporal concepts in virtue of which the experiences are not conclusive

---

[6] For an early, clear statement of this point, see F. Brentano *Sensory and Noetic Consciousness*, ed. O. Kraus, tr. L. McAlister (London: Routledge and Kegan Paul, 1981), p. 38.

for application of the concepts. In the nature of the case, this must be something more than a disposition to judge the temporal content as a function of the temporal content of an experience (or any sequence of them): any sequence whatever may be misleading. How can a concept allegedly extracted from experience alone supply the idea that experience might be misleading in respect of that concept?[7] One of the motivations for outward-looking theories of these and other notions is that this dilemma is inapplicable. We argued earlier that if we can give an account of what it is to grasp the content concerning the objective, external world, we may hope to go on to explain the possibility of hallucination: it is for the subject as if this objective content obtained, but in fact it does not. If we try to proceed in the opposite, internalist, direction of explanation, the obstacles seem insurmountable.[8]

Consider two events e and e' demonstratively presented, in either memory or sense-experience, to a given thinker: suppose they are given in modes of presentation $[W,E(\ )_e]$ and $[W',E'(\ )_{e'}]$ respectively. What might be the canonical links, on an outward-looking view, of the thought that the first event was before the second? – for instance, for the thought that that person's entry to the meeting occurred before the clock struck? It could, as a first approximation, be the commitment that

[7] This question is a highly general one which could be raised about proposals in other areas too. Their failure to answer it in the temporal case produces tensions in both James and Russell, who in Lecture IX of *The Analysis of Mind* (London: Routledge and Kegan Paul, 1921) followed James in giving the specious present a crucial role in grasp of temporal concepts. In James the tension is felt when he discusses the accuracy and acuity of temporal perception; in Russell, the discussion of temporal concepts occurs in the very same chapter as that in which he mentions the sceptical hypothesis that the world came into existence five minutes ago. Neither author raises the question of whether the account of temporal concepts he endorses leaves room for the intelligibility of the possibilities he discusses.

[8] Note that we now have at least four distinguishable senses in which some type of experience may be essential to the possession of a concept: (i) that type of experience may be mentioned in the account of mastery of the concept (observational shape concepts); (ii) an object's falling under the concept may have to be explained as its having the disposition, in certain circumstances, to produce experiences of a specified sort (secondary qualities); in the last two cases, the account of possession of the concept may say that in some cases (sense iii) or all cases (sense iv), occurrence of an experience of a certain kind is conclusively sufficient for judgement that the concept applies to an object presented in a given way.

(T)   if the subject's perceptual and memory mechanisms
      are functioning properly, and he attends to the events
      in normal circumstances, he has the impression that
      $[W, E(\ )_e]\hat{\ }<before>\hat{\ }[W', E'(\ )_{e'}]$.

This perceptual account of grasp of a temporal relation is free
of the dimensional complexities which entered the discussion
of observational contents three chapters back. Observational
concepts of objects may concern their shape in three dimensions,
while the peripheral organs whose stimulation causes the
experiences relevant to judgements involving the concepts have
a two-dimensional surface. It is this difference which makes
room for the possibility that two objects with different three-
dimensional shape cause the same experience in normal
external and internal circumstances. But time is one-dimen-
sional, and our perceptual and memory mechanisms are
sensitive to differences in time of stimulation; so there is no
difference of dimension here. Correspondingly, in a characterization of minimally functioning perceptual and memory
mechanisms in the case of impressions of temporal precedence,
we would not need any analogue of the earlier requirement
about projection classes.

   If, in our actual circumstances, someone has the impression
that the person's entry into a room occurred before the clock
struck, in circumstances in which the antecedent of (T) is
fulfilled, then the entry did occur before the striking.[9] But the
fulfilment of this canonical commitment is not generally
sufficient for the holding of the truth conditions of which it is a
commitment. This possibility is often realized: that external
conditions are normal, a properly functioning subject has the
impression that a distant explosion he hears occurs after a
flash, and yet the opposite is true, since light travels faster than

[9] We should not also say that: if the antecedent conditions are met and the
impression is not obtained, then the thought is not true: the events may be too close in
time for us to discriminate them unaided, but still one is before the other. This case is
partially analogous to an observational concept *square*, say, when predicated of
microscopically small objects. Alternatively, we could understand 'before' here as
'noticeably before': then if the antecedent conditions are met and the impression is not
obtained, the thought is not true. In either case, of course, this is but part of what is
involved in grasp of <before>, since that concept must, like that of spatial relations
between things, be allowed to have application to unperceived events.

sound. If canonical commitments are to determine truth conditions, then we need something other than (T).

It seems very much a matter for empirical investigation which events are ones impressions of whose temporal order will be misleading. So it would be wrong to try to circumscribe *a priori* some restricted class to which (T) is to apply: there is no class of which it is *a priori* true that it applies. It is also unpromising to say that (T) is fine, but must instead be taken as an account of the canonical commitments of the content that the subject's *perception* of the one event to precede the perception of the other. This is not giving us an account of the temporal relations between the objective events; and if, as seems plausible, a being can have concepts of these temporal relations between objective events without having concepts of such mental events as perceptions, the proposal is not helping us on the way.

A better account of the canonical commitment of one who judges that $[W, E(\ )_e]\char`^<before>\char`^[W', E'(\ )_{e'}]$ is this:

> if (1) a subject's perceptual and memory mechanisms are functioning properly and (2) he is so located that signals from e and e' (associated with the corresponding modes of presentation) take the same length of time to reach him, then he has the impression that $[W, E(\ )_e]\char`^<before>\char`^[W', E'(\ )_{e'}]$.

A subject may tacitly take it for granted that the antecedents (1) and (2) of this conditional are fulfilled, when in fact they are not. As before, no ability to think of or to formulate this conditional is required on the part of the subject. The condition states the commitments of the thinker, commitments which can be manifested in the circumstances under which a judgement of the content is withdrawn. This specification does not rule out the possibility that very many of the subject's impressions of temporal precedence are misleading. Nor does it require that there be some special class which could not be misleading. Because temporal notions enter clause (2), we again have a case of local holism at this basic level. We will be able to test someone's grasp of temporal notions only in the presence of auxiliary hypotheses concerning his temporal beliefs.[10]

It is hard to believe that some of the experiences of time I have mentioned *must* be possible for any being who has temporal concepts. John Campbell mentioned in discussion the possibility of a "stroboscopic world" which is illuminated by a flash every twenty seconds, say. In this world there need not be any experiences of motion. There would indeed be impressions that such-and-such happened one flash ago. But perhaps not even something like that is necessary to the possession of the concept of the past? Could there not exist a being who is capable only of impressions that such-and-such happened in the past, and who organizes these impressions by considerations of continuity, causality and coherence into a history of a continuing world? Whether or not this is possible, what should we take as *required* by possession of concepts of temporal relations and of the past?

What does seem to be required is possession of a faculty which produces mental states in a certain way: a mental state with one content rather than another is produced because the subject was formerly in a mental state systematically related to the first content. What makes a content a past-tense content is the answerability, in complex and multifarious ways, of judgements of the content to the deliverances of such a faculty. Even if the faculty just delivers dispositions to judge, rather than impressions of precedence, we still have in it an instance of an outward-looking model: because the faculty is required to meet a condition which mentions the mental states the subject *formerly* enjoyed, what individuates past-tense contents is in part a matter of their relations to what really happened in the past. The concept of the past might, then, be called *faculty-dependent*: that is, there is a faculty, more specific than one described as the ability to judge certain contents, which has to be mentioned in an account of what it is to judge an arbitrary content about the past. The concept of universal quantification, by contrast, is not faculty-dependent: if what we said about it earlier is roughly right, there is no faculty more specific than the capacity to judge certain contents which has to be

---

[10] Relativity Theory of course forces further relativization in some of these formulations: I have been outlining a naive, non-relativistic conception.

mentioned in the account of what it is to judge an *arbitrary* content containing universal quantification.

There seem to be problems – analogous to those of the extreme empiricist – if we try to give an account of possession of the concept of the past without mention of a faculty causally sensitive to the holding of states of affairs it is used to present. Suppose a subject has impressions of the form: event e_1 bears R to event e_2. He works out, as far as he can, an ordering of events by this relation R, on the supposition that it is linear. Perhaps he also uses events bearing R to the present to explain how things are now. But as before, we can ask him whether it is conceivable that his impressions of R are mistaken or not? If it is not conceivable, R is hardly the temporal relation of precedence. If it is conceivable, then we can ask how our subject does conceive of this relation: since any set of impressions of it may be misleading, his answer has to appeal to something outside the internal relations of the members of the set to one another. The point of giving an outward-looking model is precisely that it does make such an appeal.

In moving on to that part of the account which deals with, *inter alia*, thought about inaccessibles, I will mention such particular temporal and spatial relations as *one pace from* and *a few moments before* solely for purposes of exposition. But any relations impressions of which are delivered by a spatially or temporally sensitive faculty could serve the argument.

In giving the second part of the account, we have to say how the truth conditions of thoughts about inaccessibles are determined by their relations to other contents. The form of account I will be defending can be called *three-tier*. On the bottom tier, there are the canonical links for the contents about accessibles we have just been discussing. On the second tier up, there are *(a)* the truth conditions which we have been arguing are determined by these canonical links, and *(b)* various features to be elaborated concerning our conception of the inaccessible places and times. On the third tier are the truth conditions for contents concerning the inaccessible: I will be arguing that these truth conditions are determined by the two occupants of the second tier. These claims can be diagrammed:

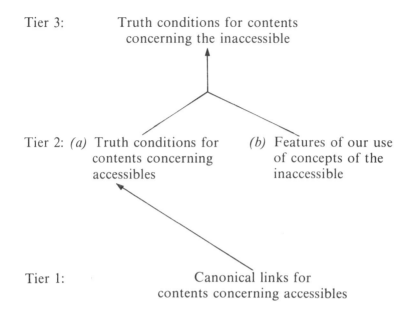

Tier 3:   Truth conditions for contents
            concerning the inaccessible

Tier 2: *(a)* Truth conditions for   *(b)* Features of our use
             contents concerning   of concepts of the
             accessibles   inaccessible

Tier 1:   Canonical links for
                            contents concerning accessibles

Many different three-tier accounts conform to this general
pattern: they vary in their descriptions of the nature and details
of the relations of determination represented by the arrows.
We still have to discuss: component *(b)* of Tier 2; Tier 3; and the
relations between the Tiers 2 and 3.

What is it to have the conception of an inaccessible place?
Let us first consider accessible places. We argued in Chapter 2
that an object's being square will, in normal external circumstances, explain the range of experiences of a minimally
functioning perceiver mentioned in the canonical commitments
of the thought that the object, presented in a certain way, is
square. Consider the thought 'One pace from here, there is
something observably square'. Here a pace is taken to be an
observationally determinable rough measure of distance.
Again, there being something observably square one pace from
here can explain a range of perceptual impressions as of there
being such a thing one pace from here. A similar point holds for
the content 'A few moments before now, it was raining', where
'a few moments ago' is taken as a roughly bounded, repeatedly
identifiable interval of time: for us, the propositional

impression here is likely (but not necessarily) to be accompanied by a memory image. In the case of this temporal content, it is the holding of the relation of being a few moments before between a time at which it was raining and the present which is causally explanatory of the impression.

The very same relations, those of being a few moments before or of being one pace from, which enter these causally explanatory conditions also hold between pairs of inaccessible times and places respectively. The ancestrals of these relations also relate inaccessible to accessible places and times. There may be a temptation to say that a relation which agrees with that of being one pace from on the accessible places, but disagrees with it on some inaccessibles, could equally be regarded as causally explanatory of our impressions. But that would be wrong. The spatial relation which explains our impressions is that of being one pace from *tout court*, and not some Goodman-like variant differing on inaccessibles. The point here is precisely the one made by Shoemaker when he remarks that if, in some respects, a human being is like a meter for detecting the property F, then the property F must be fit to feature in causal explanations, and not be grue-like: for in detecting instances of the property, the human being is responding in ways causally explained by the instantiation of the property F.[11] The same holds for the human detection of spatial and temporal relations.

A thought can concern a place 10^{20} paces away if a thinker can use in his thought some mode of presentation which requires the place to which it refers to be 10^{20} iterations of the relation of being one pace in a given direction away from his present location. We have just been arguing that the thinker can, via perception, latch on to the relation of being one pace from: there we were offering an account of one of the occupants of the middle tier of our three-tier model, the occupant which we argued is determined by the canonical links of observational contents. What of the other occupant of the second tier? On this we need to say how a thinker can conceive

---

[11] See the final section of his paper 'Projecting the Unprojectible', reprinted in his *Identity, Cause and Mind* (Cambridge: C.U.P., 1984).

of 10^{20} iterations of a relation of which he is capable of thinking.

An inaccessible place is conceived as standing in a network of spatial relations which are identical with those in which other places, both accessible and inaccessible, may stand to one another and to the original place. The place 10^{20} paces in a given direction from here is conceived as standing in exactly the same relation to the place 5×10^{19} paces away as the latter is conceived as standing to the place here. This conception of a network of spatial relations involves the number of paces between places functioning as a distance metric, and the acknowledgement of the applicability of laws mentioning distance indifferently to inaccessible and to accessible places. So, for instance, a theory quantifying over inaccessible places would not be expected to be a conservative extension of a theory quantifying, amongst places, only over the accessible: and in fact of course the distribution of matter at inaccessible places has gravitational effects on accessible places.

Do these points about possession of a conception of a network of spatial relations really determine the reference of terms referring to inaccessibles? If they do, how is the fact to be reconciled with the evident possibility that someone's use of terms for places and times may agree with ours on the accessibles and some of the inaccessibles, but diverge elsewhere? Up to '10^{20} paces from here' in any given direction, his use may agree with ours, but by '$10^{20} + 1$ paces from here' he may mean what we mean by '$10^{20} + 2$ paces from here'; and so on. There are apparently two ways this could come about. He may use numerical terms differently from us in such contexts; or the extension of 'one pace from' over 10^{20} paces away may be what we call two paces. Intuitively we want to say that such a case does not undermine the determination claim we were making. The possibility is just one in which the denotational system is irregular relative to ours: it ought to be possible to formulate the determination claim in a way that filters out irrelevant linguistic irregularity. The challenge posed by the question is to give a criterion for distinguishing such relative linguistic irregularity in such a way that the determination claim is not trivialized.

It is a partial response to this challenge simply to remark that a thinker with an irregular language will hold theories which are reconcilable with theories formulable in our own language by reconstrual of predicates, in Quine's sense.[12] In these examples, the remark is clearly correct: but it is only a partial solution because we need to give an argument for saying that theories in the language thought to be irregular *need* reconstruing, rather than being taken at face value. If we accept Reichenbach's constraint that 'universal', undetectable forces alleged to operate on all bodies in a given region are to be set to zero, some theories in the 'irregular' language would have to be reconstrued.[13] For example, a theorist using the irregular language will assert that it takes a body on which no non-universal forces are acting twice as long to travel from what he describes as '$10^{20} + 1$' to '10^{20}' paces away as it does to travel from that second place to what he describes as '$10^{20} - 1$' paces away. It seems, though, that setting universal forces to zero does not determine a unique metric.[14] Presumably we should say: only insofar as a metric is determined (up to positive linear transformations) by some constraints or other and our theorist using the apparently irregular language is violating them is *linguistic* reconstrual forced upon us. If more than one metric really is consistent with all acceptable constraints on a physical theory, then our 'irregular' language user may just be using a different metric. The content-based considerations of this section obviously cannot dissolve these substantive issues in the philosophy of space and time.

There have been two elements in this account of thought about the inaccessible. One element was the argument about causation, to the effect that the very same relation perceived to hold between some accessibles also holds between inaccessibles (and its ancestral links accessibles with inaccessibles). The other element was an account of the general conception of space and time. Neither element is dispensable. The causal

[12] 'On Empirically Equivalent Systems of the World', *Erkenntnis* **9** (1975), pp. 312–328.

[13] H. Reichenbach, *The Philosophy of Space and Time* (New York: Dover edition, 1958), p. 13ff.

[14] H. Putnam *Philosophical Papers, Volume 2: Mathematics, Matter and Method* (Cambridge: C.U.P., 1975), p. 81ff.

point about the relation 'one pace from' does not by itself suffice as an account: the mere existence of such a relation does not by itself explain how we conceive of it, how we latch on to it in thought. Conversely, to conceive of a system of spatial and temporal relations does not ensure that anything answers to one's conception. The conception has in some way to be linked to the thinker's perceptible environment if it is to be instantiated. So both elements of the present account are needed. Without the first, we would have no account at the level of thought at all; without the second, we would not have anything of the right sort for the putative thought to be about. An outward-looking account of certain contents about accessibles has been essential in developing this second element.

The two elements of the account also dovetail. The obtaining of a distant condition together with the truth of auxiliary hypotheses can causally explain local evidence: but the distant condition is also conceived of as one that can obtain independently of the existence of any local or recent evidence for it. If the distant condition were thought of as one that does not obtain independently of some evidence-yielding auxiliary hypothesis obtaining, then the condition could not be said to *explain* the existence of some objective evidence (or other) bearing on it; for then it would be *a priori* that there is some such evidence if the condition obtains.

Acceptance of principles and a general conception has to play a similar role in the account of what makes it the case that it is one observational concept rather than another which is being predicated of something at an inaccessible location. It may be initially tempting to say that if someone already refers to inaccessible places, and uses the predicate 'square' for the observational concept of being square in the case of accessible square things, then he must mean what we do by 'There is a flat, square lump of matter 10^{20} paces from here in that direction'. But there is no "must" about it at the linguistic level, since (once again) he may mean by 'square' for things 10^{15} or more paces away what we mean by 'round'. If he were to employ this deviant meaning, it would be reflected in his answers to such questions as 'Can a rectangle 10^{20} paces away be totally covered by smaller squares of some uniform size?', in a suitable context of auxiliary hypotheses about his background beliefs. This context is important: a negative answer to this particular question put to him is not by itself conclusive for deviancy in his meaning of 'square' – the deviancy may be in his use of 'totally cover'. But that could be independently confirmed too. All we need to rely on here is this: for any pair of rival hypotheses and given constant background beliefs, there are some conceivable circumstances in which those rivals have different detectable consequences. It does not contradict this that any actual body of evidence is consistent with each rival hypothesis if we are allowed to vary the auxiliary hypotheses. All that is required is that the whole set of content hypotheses – the hypotheses about content in inaccessible cases and the auxiliary hypotheses about content and belief – be determinately ascribable. When the full range of dispositions to accept theoretical claims are consistent with straight-line projection of the meaning of 'square' from the accessible cases, and if no rival interpretation fits equally well, we can say: the same property of objects, of being square, is sometimes thought to apply locally, and sometimes inaccessibly.

Though some places are absolutely inaccessible to us or to our distant ancestors, accessibility is a matter of degree: there is no sharp boundary separating the accessible from the inaccessible places. It would then be very surprising – if not incoherent – were there to be a sharp distinction within the account of mastery of a given concept between its application in accessible and its application in inaccessible cases. But in fact there is no such sharp distinction in the account just outlined. The outline of what is involved in possession of concepts of inaccessible places – the general conception involving networks of distance relations, and their role in laws – is needed equally in an account of mastery of accessible but currently unperceived places. The points about observational concepts instantiated at inaccessible places and times also equally apply to accessible but unperceived instances.[15] Consider a concept differing from *square* at any given time only

---

[15] The positive outline I have offered has not, though, been simply an uncritical analogical extension from our grasp of thoughts about currently unperceived accessible places.

in its application to unperceived instances: in the nature of the case, the difference between grasp of it and of *square* will not come out in rational responses to observed cases. To explain what is involved in our using *square* rather than some such variant, one will have to mention the same sort of fact as we did in the description of projection to the inaccessible: dispositions to accept various non-observational claims. The distinction, within an account of mastery, between the cases in which we need to mention such theoretical dispositions and those in which we do not, is not that between the accessible and the inaccessible: it is that between the perceived and the unperceived, and this is not (for a given thinker) in the same way a matter of degree.

What is the relation of the three-tier account to the truth-value links? An instance of a spatial truth-value link is the biconditional

> '10^{20} paces in that direction is a spherical object' is true if and only if an utterance or thought 'There's a spherical object here' is true when evaluated with respect to the context of 10^{20} paces in the indicated direction.[16]

This example has temporal analogues for past times: both sorts of examples are instances of more general principles, which we will take as the truth-value links.[17] It seems clear that acceptance of these links cannot fully elucidate what it is to have the conception of inaccessible places and times, since understanding of the right-hand side of such a biconditional requires a thinker already to possess that conception.[18] The

---

[16] For the distinction between evaluating a sentence with respect to a context and uttering it in a context, see David Kaplan, 'On the Logic of Demonstratives', *Journal of Philosophical Logic* **8** (1978), pp. 81–98.

[17] For discussion of these links, see M. Dummett 'The Reality of the Past' repr. in *Truth and Other Enigmas* (London: Duckworth, 1978); J. McDowell, 'On "The Reality of the Past"', in *Action and Interpretation*, ed. C. Hookway and P. Pettit (Cambridge: C.U.P., 1979); and C. Wright, *Wittgenstein's Philosophy of Mathematics* (London: Duckworth, 1978).

[18] These remarks are for the most part consistent with the views of McDowell, *op. cit.* But in the case of places, he holds that the truth-value links do point to ways in which, by travelling, a thinker can check whether truth conditions obtain (p. 133): so that in this case 'appeal to truth-value links yields an effective justification for continuing to use

three-tier account should rather be regarded as aiming to explain why the truth-value links are a correct description of the contents they mention. It aims to give that in virtue of which those links hold.

Consider now someone who does have the conception of inaccessible places. Can we then say that the thought that there is something spherical, of observable size, at one such specified place is the thought that if suitable environmental conditions for perception are met, properly functioning humans would perceive something spherical to be there? It seems clear that this counterfactual theory is incompatible with the point which Dummett has so often emphasized, that counterfactuals cannot be barely true.[19] We think of a condition 'If someone went to such-and-such place, he would have an experience as of something spherical there' as true partly in virtue of there *being* something spherical there. On the counterfactual theory being considered, this condition of there being something spherical there in turn receives a counterfactual explanation: and so the original counterfactual is after all barely true on this theory. The three-tier account avoids this embarrassment. It attempts to say how it can be that there is a certain property, say that of being spherical, which is capable of entering into causal explanations, and whose possession by something at a given place is required for a particular thought to be true: and that is a categorical condition capable of grounding a counterfactual.

In fact it is difficult even to give an initially tenable formulation of the counterfactual theory without running up against these problems. We can conceive of an arrangement in which if, counterfactually, normal perceptual conditions for

---

the notion of truth conditions in a theory of meaning'. In explaining this he uses the notion of what the thinker could in principle do. In the case of extremely distinct places, this 'in principle' would have to cover travelling faster than light. But we do not, in assessing predications of nearby places, consider what would be the case were fundamental laws of nature different: our assignments of truth values would be very different from our actual assignments were we to do so. This suggests that our grasp of the existence of very distant inaccessible places is prior to what we are prepared to say that we could in principle do (where the notion is used in McDowell's way), rather than conversely. See also the earlier discussion of Hintikka on quantification.

[19] See 'What is a Theory of Meaning? (II)', *op. cit.*

humans were fulfilled, there would no longer be anything spherical at the place in question: this does not mean that actually there is nothing spherical there. To add to the antecedent of the proffered counterfactual the clause 'without the fulfilment of environmental conditions for perception affecting whether there is something spherical there' presumes upon prior understanding of the notion of there being something spherical there, something which is not then explained by the counterfactual; while to omit such a clause results in insufficiency. These considerations seem to apply however complex are the counterfactuals offered.

According to the three-tier account, a content such as '10^{20} paces in that direction there is something spherical, of observable size' can be true even though we cannot recognize it as true. What gives the content the truth condition it has is: a sensitivity in our perceptual judgements in local cases which determines the relation 'is one pace from'; features of our theoretical claims which determine one mode of projection from accessible to inaccessible cases; and comparable points for the property of being spherical. This intelligibility of the truth condition's holding undetectably has not here been derived from acceptance of the law of bivalence. Whether what, on the three-tier view, makes it intelligible could ultimately be explained without implicit commitment to bivalence would need further investigation. In particular, the issue would have to be addressed of whether the legitimacy of introducing a classical notion of negation is implicit for objective contents concerning objects in space and time. But even if it is so implicit, the present point stands: the argument here for the intelligibility of verification-transcendent contents about inaccessibles has not proceeded *via* a premise of bivalence.

There are of course conditions of intelligible projection, and some of them can be characterized by reference to alleged projections which violate them. To someone who thinks that we can move from our conception of owned pains to unowned pains, we will be likely to reply that it is *a priori* that each pain is a pain of some subject or other, however this apparent ownership or the nature of the subject is to be analyzed. The three-tier account does not apparently violate analogous principles: inaccessible spherical material objects, for instance, are still required to exist at some place or other, and in the case of singular predications of objects, some account is offered of why it is one place rather than another which the truth condition concerns. In another kind of illegitimate projection, no theory is or could be offered of why one rather than another projection from the unproblematic cases is supposed to be correct. A believer in absolute space in the sense in which Newton believed in it may suppose that we can project from detectable changes of place to absolutely undetectable changes of place. But he can give no account – I am tempted to write 'absolutely no account' – of what would make it the case that, for instance, a thinker in using vocabulary allegedly for absolute spatial location, is talking about that rather than, say, location relative to a frame of reference moving at uniform velocity in the alleged absolute space. We have here two sides of one and the same coin. One side is the fact that there are no consequences of hypotheses about location in absolute space which are not also equally consequences of hypotheses, suitably adjusted, concerning location in the imagined uniformly moving frame of reference. The other side is that there is nothing a thinker could do, however sophisticated his theories, to manifest that he is sensitive to absolute spatial distinctions rather than to those drawn relative to the alleged moving frame of reference within it. These are two sides of the same coin, because one form such manifestation could take, were the distinction to make sense, would be to accept empirical hypotheses which are consequences of one absolute spatial distinction rather than another. But there are no such consequences. The projection to inaccessible, and of course *relative*, places has not had this sort of vacuity: the distance he takes to separate him from a given inaccessible place is empirically constrained.

If this chapter and our earlier discussion of observational contents is correct, then there is a distinctive way of arguing for realism about spatial and temporal contents concerning observational notions. It is not the only way of arguing for realism about some class of contents: I suggested a different way for universal quantificational contents. But the existence of a way special to these spatio-temporal contents might, without involving any confusion between ontological and semantic issues, justify the view that there is a distinctive case to be made for realism concerning certain contents about the natural world.[20]

[20] Dummett has always clearly insisted upon the distinctness of the ontological and semantic *issues*: see, for instance, *Frege: Philosophy of Language* First Edition, *op. cit.* pp. 507–8, and the Preface of *Truth and Other Enigmas, op. cit.* pp. xxiv–xxix. In the latter passages he is criticizing P.F. Strawson's remarks as chairman in the *Proceedings of the Aristotelian Society* 77 (1976/7), pp. 15–21. The role of causal explanation in the account of the present chapter suggests that the case that can be made for semantic realism about certain contents concerning the natural spatio-temporal world may not extend beyond that world. This reflection may cast some of Strawson's conclusions – not necessarily his arguments – in a more favourable light than that in which they are placed by Dummett.

6

Negation and Existentials

I have taken realism to be the claim that contents can be true without our being able to verify that they are true. Acknowledgment of the intelligibility of a classical negation operator is often regarded as a test of the entitlement of a theory of content to be called realistic.[1] On our official characterization of realism, this claim about negation is not trivial.[2] If the claim about negation is correct, it will take hard work to show that it is a consequence of the characterization of realism in terms of verification-transcendent truth. This chapter makes a start on just one part of the task. More particularly, I will be drawing on the account in the preceding chapters of grasp of certain verification-transcendent contents in moving towards a theory of what is involved in grasping classical negation. As before, our task is not one of reducing or analyzing a concept – who would attempt that in the case of negation? Our task is rather to supply a theory of what it is to be capable of judging contents built up using the given concept of classical negation.

It might be objected that if we really already have an account of grasp of classical truth conditions for a class of contents, no

---

[1] '. . . it *is* a requirement on realism that the classical two-valued constants can meaningfully be introduced. Since every statement is determinately either true or not, it must be *possible* to introduce a negation ~ such that ~A is true just in case A is not true, even if this is not the negation which we ordinarily employ, or even the most useful one to employ.' *Truth and Other Enigmas*, p. 274.

[2] As McDowell has emphasized: see his 'Truth Conditions, Verificationism and Bivalence' in *Truth and Meaning, op. cit.*

further genuine problem can arise about grasp of the negations of those contents. The idea that only pseudo-problems remain might start from the point that in grasping a classical truth condition, one necessarily grasps its negation. This generalizes a remark of Geach's: 'Surely what I exercise in using the term "not red" is simply the concept *red*: knowing what *is* red and knowing what *is not* red are inseparable – *eadem est scientia oppositorum*.'[3] The natural image to invoke here is that of a line dividing a plane surface: there can be no such thing as knowing where the dividing line lies but being in a position to know of only one of the two sides what shape it has. Knowing the truth condition for something is equally knowing its falsity condition, on the most fundamental notion of falsity: one knows where the dividing line lies in logical space.

But these correct points do not show that we were dealing with a mere pseudo-problem about negation. To have, for instance, an account of mastery and manifestation of a content whose truth condition is in effect that all the commitments in a certain set are fulfilled is not yet to have such an account for a content whose truth condition is that not all those commitments are fulfilled. Nor does the truth condition of a sentence determine the nature of a negation operating on it: constructive negations may be applied to a classical content. We still have the question 'How is grasp of *classical* negation manifested?'

Let A be any content whose canonical commitments determine its truth conditions, in one of the ways we have already discussed. Then if an operator $ is to be classical negation it is constitutively required that:

(N) $\ulcorner \$A \urcorner$ is judged true when any one of the canonical commitments of A is discovered to fail.

(N), like the other conditions displayed below, is to be understood as requiring that what it says holds also in counterfactual circumstances in which $ retains its actual sense. Without this understanding, the displayed conditions could not distinguish negation from various other conceivable operators extensionally equivalent to it, such as '!': for any sentence A, $\ulcorner !A \urcorner$ has the same sense as '$\sim A$ and the earth is

[3] *Mental Acts* (London: Routledge and Kegan Paul, 1957), p. 25.

round'. It is the actions of subjects in counterfactual circumstances in which they no longer accept that the earth is round which will discriminate between the hypothesis that their \$ means $\sim$ and the hypothesis that it means !.

Is it circular to use the notion of commitments *failing* in an account of grasp of classical negation? We will take in turn the two cases we have considered in more detail, starting with observational predications of demonstratively presented objects. Here one of the canonical commitments fails when the object is presented in a perceptual experience which is not of a type which could, in normal circumstances, be produced by something falling under the observational concept. In these circumstances (N) requires that the thinker be disposed to judge the negation of the observational predication, should the question arise in thought. So (N) requires that the thinker be sensitive in his observational judgements to the distinction between those perceptual experiences which could, and those which could not, be produced in normal circumstances by something falling under the observational concept.

In describing the distinction to which the thinker must be sensitive, we have just used the notion of negation: but that is we, the theorists, using it, not him. The position is similar to that in which we, from the outside, use conjunction in describing the rules to which a connective must conform if it is to be counted as conjunction; this does not make the account of what it is to grasp conjunction circular. As noted, our task is a theory of grasp of a concept: since that is our task, rather than definition of the concept, it is quite legitimate for us to use the concept itself in elucidating grasp of that very concept.

We also considered present-tensed unrestricted universal quantification over concrete objects: here the canonical commitments were of the form 'If there's an F at the place (if any) bearing R to π, then it's G'. So for that case (N) will relate the mastery of negation of such a universally quantified condition to the failure of one of these commitments: the negation is judged if one of the commitments is found to fail. If our thinker can respond to the failure of one of these conditions as (N) requires, he must certainly have grasped what it is for an arbitrary F not to be G – a negated condition. So we must be able to give an account of that grasp if (N) is to succeed. But none of these negations is the negation of a universal quantification. And it was grasp of the negation of a universal quantification which was under consideration: so there is not a circularity of the sort which would result if grasp of a negated universal quantification were explained in terms of grasp of a negated universal quantification *tout court*.

(N) is clearly not sufficient for $ to be classical negation. An operator which means 'it is establishably false that' would also conform to (N). But on the classical conception, a universal quantification may be false though not establishably false. So too may a present-tense predication of an observational concept if auxiliary conditions prevent testing of that thought now or at any later moment. We must also add that it is constitutively required that

(DN) the thinker is, after reflection, prepared to accept the equivalence of $\ulcorner \$\$A \urcorner$ with A, or at least manifests in his inferential practice the immediate consequences of such acceptance.[4]

'It is establishably false that' does not conform to (DN): A is not equivalent to the establishable falsity of the establishable falsity of A. A simple case would be that in which we know from auxiliary hypotheses that there can be no further evidence as to whether the canonical commitments of A are fulfilled. Then it would be establishably false that it is establishably false that A; but this does not entail that A is true.

It may be objected that if someone has to reflect before accepting a content, acceptance of that content should not be required by a constitutive account of the concepts from which that content is composed; and does not (DN) violate this? The argument behind the principle of this objection is presumably that concepts (modes of presentation) are individuated by considerations of informativeness. If it takes some reflection to

---

[4] Some realists may allow contents which are neither true nor false ("which have value N", let us say). We then have to be careful to disambiguate 'equivalence': do we mean the validity of the biconditional $A \leftrightarrow \sim\sim A$, or the mutual semantic consequence of A with $\sim\sim A$? These are different. Suppose $\sim A$ has value N when A does, and that $B \leftrightarrow C$ also has value N when B and C do: then $A \leftrightarrow \sim\sim A$ will have value N when A does. But it can still be the case that under all valuations A is true iff $\sim\sim A$ is true. The realist who admits truth-value gaps and wants to use (DN) as we do should then mean by 'equivalence' mutual semantic consequence, rather than validity of the biconditional.

realize that a content is true, then before reflection that content can be informative. Now this does show that immediate acceptance cannot be required for grasp of the content. But (DN) requires only grasp after reflection. In doing so, it is in step with what we will need to say in many other cases. If someone has made no mistakes, we require him to give a certain answer to the question 'What is $37 + 84$?' if he is to have the concept of addition rather than some other concept. But we do not require him to be able to give the answer without reflection.

Now consider a content whose truth condition is determined by its spectrum of canonical commitments, as outlined in the above chapters; and suppose that it has a determinate truth value. Suppose too that we have an operator $ applied to that content, and that $ conforms to both (N) and (DN). *If* $ operates on truth values, then it must have the truth table of classical negation. From (DN) $ has to have as its semantical value a function whose composition with itself is the identity function; and from (N) it cannot itself be the identity function. This leaves only the function which maps true to false and *vice versa*.

This needs a *caveat*. Strictly we have not argued that anything with a determinate classical (*i.e.* possibly verification-transcendent) truth condition must be determinately either true or false: admission of recognition-transcendent truth conditions does not obviously result in commitment to bivalence.[5] So the argument just given leads only to the conclusion that *when* the embedded sentences have truth values, such an operator $ must behave as classical negation.

That $ *can* be interpreted as operating on the truth value of a verification-transcendent condition is of course a necessary condition of applying the argument about negation. If we did not have some independent account, of the sort we aimed to give earlier for such particular cases as universal quantification, of grasp of verification-transcendent conditions, then we would have no argument here for taking some sign or thought-constituent as classical negation. So the argument of the preceding paragraphs is *not* an example of the view that grasp

[5] See note 2 of this chapter.

of realistic contents is manifested solely by the application of classical logic to those contents. The view I am defending is rather that the inferential transitions between A and $\sim\sim A$ play an essential but not exhaustive role in giving negation its classical interpretation. According to the theory defended here, the realistic status of the content of 'All F's are G' is established without any mention of application of the classical negation rules to it.

Is the present view one on which a set of inference rules fully determine the meaning of classical negation? On the one hand, intuition strongly supports the idea that there must be something in such a claim of determination: one wonders what else besides such inference rules can fix the meaning of negation. On the other hand, it is a delicate matter to formulate precisely the sense in which this claim of determination is true. Dummett has given this plausible necessary condition for a set of inference rules to determine the meaning of a set of logical constants:

> the condition for the correctness of an assertion made by means of a sentence containing a logical constant must always coincide with the existence of a deduction, by means of those rules of inference, to that sentence from correct premises none of which contains any of the logical constants in question.[6]

The double negation rules, and indeed the full set of classical negation rules, fail this plausible condition: negations of atomic sentences can certainly be correct without being deducible from correct negation-free premises.[7] Someone of a more constructivist frame of mind might widen Dummett's necessary condition to allow deductions from decidably correct negated atomic sentences.[8] But this route is closed to me for several reasons. One reason is that it is not clear that

---

[6] *Elements of Intuitionism, op. cit.* p. 363.

[7] Suppose there were a set S of negation-free formulae of the predicate calculus such that the negation of an atomic formula were deducible from S. Assign all atomic sentences the value true, and give the universal extension to all atomic predicate and relation letters. All formulae in S will come out true under this assignment, while the negated atomic formula is false under it. This would contradict the soundness of classical logic: so the original supposition is false.

[8] This constructivist has to unify the negation of decidable sentences with the negation of undecidable sentences: but he could adapt to his purposes analogues of the arguments given later in this chapter.

even present tense observational predications of perceptually presented objects are decidable, given the commitment account and the local holisms we discussed. A second reason is that taking this route is not going to yield a treatment of negations of predications of observational concepts of objects at inaccessible locations.

A more promising route is to introduce a broader notion: that of meaning being determined not by inference rules, but by *transition* rules. Every inference rule is a transition rule, but not every transition rule is an inference rule. A transition rule is any normative rule which determines when a given type of content may reasonably be judged. To take a now familiar case: a transition rule may specify or determine that a minimally functioning perceiver who in normal circumstances experiences a presented object in a way in which a φ object could not, in those circumstances, be experienced can judge that the presented object is not φ (for observational φ). Correspondingly there will be transition rules generated by the three-tier model. What is correct in the idea that the meaning of negation is determined by inference rules is more accurately expressed by saying that its meaning is determined by *transition* rules. The account I am outlining is not just consistent with but suggests a way of elaborating the claim that the meaning of negation is determined by the transition rules governing it.[9]

Those using classical negation, unlike those using a constructive negation, will accept the content 'It could be that not all *F*'s are *G*, even though we do not and will not know of any falsifying instance or of any disproof of it'. So why did I not appeal to this fact in the account of classical negation? There are three reasons. First, it seems that the modal content is not a primitive, self-justifying principle about negation: we want rather to say that it is a consequence of the content of negation and universal quantification. Second, many other operators will also conform to the principle: we want a theory on which the classical contribution to truth conditions is *determined*. So if we mentioned the modal principle explicitly in the account,

---

[9] The role of these transition rules may be illuminatingly compared with the role of the 'language entry transitions' in Wilfrid Sellars' work: see, for example, the essays 'Is There a Synthetic *A Priori*?' and 'Some Reflections on Language Games' in his *Science, Perception and Reality* (London: Routledge and Kegan Paul, 1963).

we would need to add more. The question arises whether the additional material would not itself determine the content of classical negation (as we have argued it would if we mentioned (N) and (DN) in the cases discussed): the appeal to modality would then be redundant. Finally, it seems that someone could be using classical negation, quantification and other contents without using modal notions. No doubt it must be true that if such a thinker were introduced to modal notions, he would have to accept the modal content we mentioned. But if his negation had the classical content before he used modal notions, they should not be mentioned in the account of grasp of that content. It would not help to introduce counterfactuals concerning his acceptance were he to start to use modal notions. The antecedents of the counterfactuals would have somehow to require that his negation did not shift its content when modality was introduced. Again, the supposition that it is possible that there is no shift relies on the possibility of mastery of classical negation without grasp of modality.

What I have said so far about grasp of classical negation is at best only a fragment of an account, because (N) treats only those contents which have canonical commitments. Not all contents have such commitments: we will need something more general if we are to have an account of negation applied to those contents which do not have them. The negative content 'Not all F's are G' is just such a content. What it has is not a family of canonical commitments, but rather a family of canonical grounds. These are the conditions each one of which would refute 'All F's are G', i.e., all conditions of the form 'There is an F at the place bearing R to π, and it is not G'. The content of the double negation which is the negation of 'Not all F's are G' in turn has as its immediate commitment that none of these committing conditions just mentioned hold: it has as *its* immediate canonical commitments all contents of the form 'It's not the case that: there is an F at the place bearing R to π which is also not G'. Since, incidentally, these commitments contain two occurrences of negation, this account is not forced to identify the content 'All F's are G' with its double negation: for their *immediate* canonical commitments are not the same.

But we have still been considering only the special cases in which the contents have either canonical grounds or canonical commitments. What, for instance, of such contents as 'The slab at π is not square', where 'π' is replaced by an expression denoting an inaccessible place? I programmatically suggest this general strategy: for any content, we look at the model of how its truth condition is determined. This model must determine the boundary between the truth and falsity of the content: and we can aim to exploit the features which determine that boundary in giving for a new type of content what (N) gives in the commitment case. The idea is that (N) is an instance of a more widely applicable type of model. In pursuing this strategy, we may hope to make clear a level at which the account of mastery of negations of different kinds of content is uniform: *viz.*, that the *relation* between what stands in place of (N) for a new content and the model of how the new content's truth conditions are determined is the same as the *relation* between (N) and the commitment model. It is because of this uniformity of relation that such an account of mastery of negation need not be merely piecemeal, varying unsystematically from one type of content to another.

With partial accounts of grasp of classical negation and of universal quantification before us, a theorist might propose that we draw on them and say that existential quantification is grasped simply as an abbreviation: the proposal would be that '$\exists x \, (Fx, Gx)$' is grasped as an abbreviation of '$\sim\forall x \, (Fx, \sim Gx)$'. But of course we can equally conceive of the opposite direction of explanation, of grasp of the universal in terms of the existential. Taken as explanations of understanding – rather than as logical equivalences – it cannot be that both explanations are correct. We would need a reason for believing one over the other: that we happen to have an account of universal quantification already is not enough.

In fact there is already a place in the present scheme for a more direct description of grasp of existential quantification. We allowed that a constitutive account of contents of a given type could mention those contents' canonical *committing* conditions, their canonical grounds. The account for existential quantification can be a case in point. As in our earlier discussion of universal quantification, let us restrict attention to examples in which F and G range over observational concepts true or false of material objects. We also confine ourselves to present tense existential quantifications over material objects. The family of committing conditions, the canonical grounds, for such a quantification 'Some F is G' will then be all conditions of the form

(E)   There is at π an F which is G;

where the range of places π is conceived of as open-ended, in the way discussed in Chapter 3.

Conditions of the form (E) seem themselves to be existential: so a full account of grasp of existential quantification must explain grasp of *them* too. Consider first a sentence of the form 'There's an F here which is G'; and suppose it is uttered in a context in which the 'here' indicates a place sufficiently finely discriminated (perhaps in perception) that at most one F could occupy it. There is a natural way of taking this utterance on which no grasp of a range for the seeming existential quantifier 'there is' is required for understanding it. If a wider or narrower range of objects were alleged to be associated with the apparent existential, the variation in range would make no difference to the determination of the truth value of the utterance, which just requires the unique F at the indicated place to be G.

Now consider an arbitrary condition of the form in (E), in which the place to which there is singular reference is sufficiently finely discriminated that there can be at most one F there.[10] This can be understood as like the case containing 'here', with the sole difference that some other place is mentioned. For similar reasons, the apparent quantifier need not introduce a range. Suppose, in step with the three-tier account of Chapter 5, that a thinker has some conception of the place mentioned in our condition of the form (E); and in step with the same model, suppose too that he possesses the observational concepts F and G, and uses them in predications concerning perceived and predications concerning unperceived places. The three-tier model then supplies the materials for explaining this thinker's grasp of the condition 'There is at π an

---

[10] I am being casual about the distinction between variables over places, and variables over modes of presentation thereof. Strictly the condition must contain a singular mode of presentation of a place.

F which is *G*'. There being an *F* here which is *G* can causally explain its seeming to a subject that it is so; and such seemings would be mentioned in a statement of the canonical commitments of the content that there is an *F* here which is *G*. The same property, which holds here and which explains the impressions, can hold of the place π too. When it does, it is true that there is at π an *F* which is *G*.

We argued in the case of universal quantification that the canonical commitments determined the truth condition: we can similarly say now that an existential quantification is true just in case some one of its canonical grounds, its canonical committing conditions, holds. As in the universal case, the truth condition is implied by the holding of some one of the canonical grounds only under an additional supposition: some supposition which ensures that the thinker is disposed to acknowledge something as a genuine place just in case it is so. Without this addition, the wrong truth condition would be attributed, for reasons similar to those we discussed in the universal case. If there are places which the thinker is not disposed to acknowledge as such, then (without the addition) the truth condition determined by the canonical grounds would be too weak. The opposite problem would also arise if the thinker believes there are places which in fact there are not.

If we consider only examples in which our thinker infers an existential quantification from some singular instance which he believes, we would have equally to admit that a different, and incorrect, truth condition is also determined by the canonical grounds. This would be the incorrect truth condition for 'Some *F* is *G*' that there is some *F* which is *G* and which the thinker can specify. That this is not the correct content would be shown only in the thinker's use of existential quantification within such constructions as conditionals, subordinate proof, and the operator '. . . caused it to be the case that ___'. For instance, we may want to say that an automatic alarm was set off because there was at least one person in the museum: under the incorrect truth condition, we could not say this in all the cases we would want.

As in the universal case, there is a corresponding explanation of one of the Ramseyan phenomena. No particular alternation $(Fa \& Ga) \lor (Fb \& Gb) \lor$ . . . . containing singular recognitional or demonstrative modes of presentation is *a priori* equivalent to the quantification '$\exists x(Fx, Gx)$'; this is so because there is no *a priori* guarantee that a given class of modes of presentation of those sorts exhausts the F's which are at the places in the class of which we gave an open-ended characterization back in Chapter 3.

With the end of the present chapter, I conclude consideration in this essay of particular types of content. Even in relation to those few types I have been considering, much remains to be elucidated (and no doubt revised). But I hope the sketch has been enough to make it plausible that some adequate account of the *form* at which I have been aiming could be given. In the remainder of this essay, I consider how we might answer challenges to that general form, and I go on to apply the account in epistemology.

PART III

DOUBTS ADDRESSED

7

Objections

The most influential reason for doubting the possibility of any acceptance condition theory of content concerns the fourth Fregean property, that one and the same Thought may be judged by different subjects. If an acceptance theory is to define contents which have this property, it must answer the point that the presence of vastly different bodies of collateral information in different thinkers obstructs the delineation of any particular detailed conditions to which a thinker *must* rationally be sensitive if he is to be counted as judging a given content. Thus Quine: 'dispositions [to assent to or dissent from sentences as a result of stimulation] may be conceded to be impure in the sense of including worldly knowledge, but they contain it in a solution which there is no precipitating'.[1] Field has endorsed the objection.[2] Before I speak to it, I want to step back to make a few more general remarks on interpersonal identity of content.

We have a continuing and relatively successful practice of ascribing propositional attitudes to one another. The nature of interpersonal identity of content must be given by its role in that practice. It does not follow, though, that interpersonal identity of content bears any very close relation to the

---

[1] *Word and Object* (Cambridge, Mass.: MIT Press, 1960), p. 39.
[2] 'Logic, Meaning and Conceptual Role', *op. cit.*, and 'Mental Representation', repr. in *Readings in Philosophy of Psychology* Vol. 2, ed. N. Block (London: Methuen, 1981).

conditions for the correct utterance of belief *sentences*. The relations will not be close, for several familiar reasons. First, there are modes of presentation which are not fully captured by linguistic expressions: this is true of perceptual modes of presentation, and arguably of some observational ways of thinking of properties. Second, there are words in the language, most particularly proper names and natural kind terms, for which there is no way of thinking such that in order to understand the word, one must think of its referent (object or kind) in that particular way.[3] Third, in classifying attitudes to given contents we often need an apparatus which discriminates more finely than that which is straightforwardly made available by the natural language: Kaplan's discussion for belief contexts of the need to capture certain forms of agnosticism is one example.[4] Fourth, even when we take sentences which do fully express particular contents, the contents expressed are for many purposes sliced too finely to capture the level at which we want to characterize general features of their role in propositional attitude psychology. The relevant level is often not that of mode of presentation, nor that of entity presented by the mode of presentation; it is, in the terminology favoured in this essay, that of the kind of mode of presentation.[5]

Suppose, however, we restrict our attention for the purposes of this paragraph only to some arbitrary sentence *s* which fully determines a content, and which can be grasped by some other subject (John, say) situated as he is. In this special case, there is

[3] See, for instance, D. Wiggins, 'Identity, Designation, Essentialism and Physicalism' *Philosophia* **5** (1975), pp. 1–30.

[4] D. Kaplan, 'Quantifying In', in *Words and Objections*, ed. D. Davidson and J. Hintikka (Dordrecht: Reidel, 1969), esp. pp. 234–5.

[5] On this notion of type – not necessarily so described – see J. Perry, 'Perception, Action and the Structure of Believing', forthcoming in a *Festschrift* for Paul Grice, edited by R. Grandy and R. Warner; G. Evans, 'Understanding Demonstratives', in *Meaning and Understanding* ed. H. Parret and J. Bouvresse (De Gruyter: Berlin, 1981); C. Peacocke, 'Demonstrative Thought and Psychological Explanation', *Synthese* **49** (1981), pp. 187–217. In 'Mental Representation', Field splits up '*x* believes that *p*' into '*x* believes* *s* and *s* means that *p*', where 'believes*' expresses a relation to an internal sentence-analogue. Field says that what such a sentence means is to be given by a Tarski-style truth theory. Are truth theories which attribute the same references to the same expressions to be counted as equally good here? If so, the account seems too thin for commonsense psychology. If not, further constraints on the choice of the theory are needed.

a closer connection between interpersonal identity of content and the correct utterance of a belief sentence. For here we can say that a speaker truly utters 'John believes'$^\frown s$ iff: John believes something whose canonical acceptance conditions are the same as those of the content expressed by s on the speaker's lips. Let us call those features of the causal role of judgement of a given content in a thinker's cognitive organization which are determined by the content itself *content-determined* features. It is tempting to say that in uttering 'John believes that p', a speaker is saying that John is in a belief state whose role in John's cognitive organization is similar to that of the belief he would express in uttering this sentence sincerely: p. The remarks earlier in this paragraph suggest that the theory of content in this essay has, at least for content-determined features of a judgement's causal role and for sentences meeting our conditions on s, that tempting account as a consequence.[6]

Let us return to the person-relativity of collateral information. We tried to give an account of the distinction between a content's canonical and its non-canonical grounds and commitments; but that account by itself would hardly satisfy Quine. His position is that however sharp that account may seem, we cannot apply it with determinacy: we cannot empirically distinguish a subject who is said to be judging one content thus individuated from a subject who is judging a different content. This is Quine's argument for the point, formulated at the level of linguistic expression of content:

> Thus, to depict the difficulty in more general terms, suppose it said that a particular class Σ comprises just those stimulations each of which suffices to prompt assent to a sentence S outright, without benefit of collateral information. Suppose it said that the stimulations comprised in a further class Σ', likewise sufficient to prompt assent to S, owe their efficacy rather to certain widely disseminated collateral information, C. Now couldn't we just as well have said, instead, that on acquiring C,

---

[6] At this point – despite many other differences – my account and that of S. Stich converge: see his *From Folk Psychology to Cognitive Science* (Cambridge, Mass.: MIT Press, 1983), esp. p. 88 ff. Note that although when Stich uses the notion of causal role he means what has come to be known as "narrow" causal role, in assessing similarity of beliefs for the purposes of content-ascription he does include referential features of the belief (p. 89ff.).

men have found it convenient implicitly to change the very "meaning" of S, so that the members of Σ' now suffice outright like members of Σ? I suggest that we may say either; even historical clairvoyance would reveal no distinction, though it reveal all stages in the acquisition of C, since meaning can evolve *pari passu*. The distinction is illusory . . .[7]

But the hypothesis that Σ gives the meaning of S and the hypothesis that Σ' gives its meaning differ in their consequences. For vividness, we can use the example which Davidson mentioned to Quine, and take Σ to be the affirmative stimulus meaning of 'rabbit' and Σ' to be the affirmative stimulus meaning of 'rabbit fly'.[8] (Rabbit flies exist only in the vicinity of rabbits.) Suppose also that a subject comes to believe that rabbits cannot survive in conditions D, and yet he remembers finding rabbit flies in conditions D. Suppose we now give him a stimulation in $\Sigma' - \Sigma$ in conditions which are obviously D. If Σ' gives the meaning of S, S will still receive assent; while if Σ gives the meaning, S will not receive assent. The hypotheses differ in these counterfactual consequences. What Quine has set up is a case of underdetermination by the actual evidence. The example shows that there is no fact of the matter in the case of meaning only if we hold that there is no fact of the matter as to which of two theories differing in respect of their counterfactual consequences is true, even when those consequences are not highly theoretical. Analogous points can be made at the level of thought. In both the linguistic case and the case of thought, the counterfactual consequences of differing hypotheses about content are derived only with the use of auxiliary hypotheses about other beliefs, desires and intentions of our subject: the counterfactual difference discriminates only between the addition of one rather than the other of these meaning or content hypotheses to this background set of hypotheses.[9]

We have just given a response to a case in which it was said

---

[7] *Word and Object*, p. 38.

[8] *Ibid.*, p. 37.

[9] This is of course a reply to just one of Quine's challenges, and can hardly constitute a general refutation of indeterminacy claims: and indeed we took the content of our subject's auxiliary attitudes for granted. Quine might say that distinctions of meaning are still unempirical on the ground that if we brought about the test conditions concerning $\Sigma' - \Sigma$, S might change its meaning: so that these counterfactuals about

that even at the level of stimulus meaning, we cannot separate out the effects of collateral information. But a response of the same sort can be given to a corresponding Quinean point when the content is more theoretical. Suppose for instance we are concerned with a content which we take as ascribing a particular belief: so judging the content is governed by the rational theoretical constraints. If the content is in fact judged true by a thinker when the attributee behaves in a certain way, we can imagine an analogous Quinean challenge: why, the analogous challenge runs, should we not say that the content judged is one which has as one of its canonical grounds that the attributee behave in that very way? The corresponding reply is that we have to consider the thinker's response when he is given extensive evidence that the attributee has evidence that the given behaviour would not help but would rather hinder the attainment of his goals when the particular belief in question is true. If the thinker then no longer judges the content when the attributee behaves that way, that is evidence against the attribution mentioned in the imagined Quinean challenge. The strategy of the response is generalizable.

A related source of resistance to the present conception of content may be the fact that the notion of a canonical link is too reminiscent of the idea of criteria and noninductive evidence. Some conceptions of criteria, based on early interpretations of Wittgenstein's writings, came under heavy attack from Putnam and others.[10] Are canonical acceptance conditions anything but these discredited criteria operating under a new name? Certainly there are points of similarity. Wittgenstein wrote of 'the grounds [of our belief in a proposition], which are grammatically related to the proposition, and tell us what proposition it is'.[11] Canonical acceptance conditions are

---

assent to S show nothing about its *actual* meaning. Such a scepticism can be formulated about any notion – including that of solubility – which has dispositional components. It is a good question how it is to be met, consistently with admitting – as we must – that test conditions do sometimes affect what was to be tested. But we do not have here a special problem about meaning and content.

[10] See Putnam's 'Brains and Behavior' and other papers on the philosophy of mind in his *Philosophical Papers Volume 2: Mathematics, Matter and Method, op. cit.*

[11] *Zettel*, tr. G.E.M. Anscombe (Berkeley: University of California Press, 1970).

likewise used here in the individuation of contents. A second point of similarity is that we will also be using canonical acceptance conditions in an account of what is required specifically for *knowledge* of a given content. There was similarly mention of knowledge in the passages in which Wittgenstein introduced criteria.[12] But there are also major differences. I have emphasized the possible roles of theory in acceptance conditions, and Putnam's criticisms centred on the failure of the then current criterial accounts to leave room for it. Some criterial theorists also held the relation between the criteria and the conditions for which they are criteria to be conventional, or founded on a definition.[13] There are certainly in the present account *a priori* principles linking what is mentioned in canonical acceptance conditions with the contents for which they are acceptance conditions: but how this can be so is a special case of the general problem of *a priori* truth – there is no commitment here to a form of conventionalism. Criteria were also supposed by some to replace truth-conditional accounts of content: I have been suggesting, in the initial Conjecture, a quite different relation between substantive truth-conditional accounts and canonical acceptance conditions. It was also implicit in our earlier discussion of outward-looking theories that they, unlike the claims made by some proponents of criteria, provide no quick means of dismissing all forms of radical scepticism as incoherent.

It is quite common in the case of highly theoretical contents for a thinker first to grasp some content, and only later, after the exercise of some ingenuity and reasoning, come to think of what might be possible evidence for or against the truth of that content. So some nineteenth century physicist may have formed the conjecture that electro-magnetic waves and light consist in disturbances of the aether, which is at rest in an inertial frame of reference. It took thought to reason that if such an aether exists, then the time taken by a beam of light to

---

[12] See *The Blue Book* (New York: Anchor, 1958), p. 24, where the implication throughout is that criteria have a special relevance in answering the question 'How do you know that he has got toothache?'.

[13] Though there is more than one way of construing the passages in Wittgenstein which seem to support this: the correct interpretation may be an application to evidential relations of his views about ways human beings, as a matter of natural history, find it compelling to go on.

travel on a given round trip ought to depend on the state of motion of the laboratory apparatus relative to the aether, and hence on the orientation of that apparatus. But if the content of a hypothesis can be grasped before the thinker has worked out what might be reasons for or against accepting it, how can grasp of content be identified with grasp of canonical acceptance conditions? But the acceptance condition theorist can accommodate this kind of example. He ought to say that the canonical acceptance condition for the content that the aether exists is the same as that for the content that there is a medium the disturbances of which include electro-magnetic radiation and light rays. What one *does* have to reason out, and discovery of which is not a requirement for grasping the content, is that a positive outcome to a certain experiment *is* evidence that there is such a medium.[14] Such a recognition is no more required for grasping the content than it is required that one should be able to cite, unprompted, some highly indirect logical means of establishing a universal generalization before one can be attributed general thoughts.

It is also indisputable that there is no one way one has to think of some type of theoretical entity in order to understand a name in the language for entities of that type. Different people may think of electrons in quite different ways, but both still understand the English word 'electron': the phenomenon here is, as Putnam has said in a different connection, analogous to that for proper names – there is no one way one has to think of the city in order to understand the name 'London'. This point just emphasizes the fact that the present acceptance condition theory is an account of the nature of *thought* contents, and we have already noted that one must not assume that the thought is uniquely determined by its natural linguistic expression. To accept a theory of content which uses the idea of canonical acceptance conditions does not commit one to believing that there are interesting, detailed and specific analytic truths involving theoretical terms. Whether 'It is analytic that'$^\frown A$ is true depends on what one has to know to understand the

---

[14] To meet the objection squarely, an account of the content that there is such a medium must itself be given in terms of canonical acceptance conditions. Doing so would presumably involve giving for thoughts about the very small what we aimed to give for thoughts about the spatially and temporally inaccessible in Chapter 5.

sentence A. If different persons may think of the property denoted by a theoretical term in different ways but still understand that term, we would not expect there to be interesting analytic truths in which the theoretical term occurs essentially.

Of course it is not true that *all* indeterminacy is concentrated at the level of language. It is not as if there were a realm of thoughts, with fully determinate degrees of truth with respect to every possible situation – so that indeterminacy arises only because of looseness of association of sentences with these thoughts. To use Field's example, the Newtonian physicist's thoughts expressed using sentences containing 'mass' suffer the same indeterminacy of reference as between relativistic mass and proper mass as do the sentences he uses in expression of those thoughts.[15] It is an empirical question what indeterminacies there are and at what level they occur.

We argued earlier that an acceptance condition theory of content is consistent with certain limited forms of holism, notably those cases in which the acceptance conditions of the contents at a given level have to be specified by reference to a certain form of theory. The conception outlined here is, though, incompatible with what Dummett has called "radical holism", the doctrine, for sentences, that the sense of a sentence is to be given by the totality of ways that exist in the language for establishing its truth.[16] As Dummett says, on such a view there is no room for the idea that two thinkers, one of whom has a very rich conceptual repertoire (the rich thinker) and the other of whom (the poor thinker) does not, may nevertheless share some sentences which have the same sense.[17] Again, a corresponding point would apply to thoughts. The

[15] H. Field 'Theory Change and the Indeterminacy of Reference', *Journal of Philosophy* **70** (1973), pp. 462–81.

[16] See 'The Justification of Deduction' in *Truth and Other Enigmas, op. cit.*

[17] Dummett may seem to be rejecting this point when he remarks that it is an advantage of the radical holist's view that he can give a justification of deductive practices, *viz.* that this is simply one of our ways of establishing the truth of a given sentence, and so is *ipso facto* justified by the sense of the sentence, on that holist's conception. This remark is in tension with opposition to radical holism, for the radical holist has no right to the view that the sentence established by deduction has the *same* sense as one present prior to the introduction of the deductive inference in question. I think we should just classify this remark as a slip on Dummett's part, inconsistent as it is with the major thrust of his position.

present account of thoughts is of course committed to making sense of the idea that two thinkers, one of whom has a much richer conceptual repertoire than the other, may be capable of judging the same thought. This possibility cannot be explained in any way which presumes that, *modulo* inductive uncertainty, they judge the same contents in the same evidential circumstances. The richer thinker may employ his more extensive repertoire of concepts and auxiliary hypotheses precisely because their use in a theory allows him to predict and explain the truth of more simple contents which he could not predict and explain without them. What makes for sameness of content according to the present theory is sameness of *canonical* acceptance conditions: the richer person accepts a wider body of evidence as bearing on a given content than the poorer person only because he believes his wider evidential basis is suitably correlated with what is mentioned in the canonical acceptance conditions for the given content. If this were not a true claim about the richer person's reasons, and the difference in evidential sensitivity between the two could not be explained by differences of inductive boldness, a claim of intersubjective identity of content would seem unsustainable.

Whether someone who offers the positive outline of a theory of content I have been suggesting is really offering something which conforms to Frege's fourth property – that one and the same Thought can be judged, argued about or agreed upon by two different thinkers – depends on something which lies beyond the scope of this essay, *viz.* an account of sameness of experience type between different subjects. That notion played an essential role in the substantive theory of content for the level which had no other levels below it in the Grand Partial Ordering of contents. Interpersonal identity of experience needs much more philosophical discussion. But anyone who accepts that the subjective properties of experience are not absolutely incommunicable between thinkers is committed to thinking that there is some account of the sort needed by the present theory.

Another major source of objection to the account I have been offering is its use of the idea that a perceptual experience can justify a belief. In response to this idea, an earlier generation of coherence theorists of truth would have retorted that only a belief can justify a belief. More recently, Davidson has objected to the same idea.[18] Because perceptual experience is such a treacherous subject, even a brief discussion of this issue needs to start with a clear formulation of the claim that experiences can justify beliefs.

We will take the claim that experiences can justify beliefs to be this: that the occurrence to a subject of an experience of an object x, presented in way W as an F that is φ can justify for the subject the perceptual-demonstrative belief 'that F is φ' ($[W,F(\ )_x]\hat{}[\varphi]\hat{}[now_t]$). The 'can' leaves open for further specification the circumstances in which this possibility is realized. In this formulation of the claim, it is the occurrence of the experience itself which justifies, and not the belief that such an experience is occurring. The content of the belief justified by the experience goes beyond the experience in the sense that such an experience could occur but the content of the belief be false. The claim is not committed to the view that a subject's experiences have private features unknowable in principle by others.

In 'Empirical Content', Davidson writes that the mundane events in which we discover that some of our beliefs are true and others false should not 'be analyzed as involving evidence which is not propositional in character'.[19] I agree: and formulations of the kind just given comply with one understanding of Davidson's requirement. A visual experience has a rich propositional representational content, one which contains the representational content of the belief it justifies. The experience may have that content whether or not the subject endorses it in judgment, which he may not if he does not trust his senses. Where the present account diverges from Davidson is in the gloss with which the quotation just given continues: 'evidence which is not propositional in character – evidence which is not some sort of belief'.

A second complaint against the claim that experience can justify belief is that experience can justify belief only if it causes the belief on the subject's part that he is having an experience:

[18] See his papers 'Empirical Content', *Grazer Philosophische Studien* **16/17** (1982), pp. 471–489, and 'A Coherence Theory of Truth and Knowledge' in *Kant oder Hegel?* (Stuttgart: Klett-Cotta, 1983) ed. D. Henrich: these papers are henceforth referred to as '*EC*' and '*ACT*' respectively.
[19] *EC* p. 477.

and then, the objection runs, it is this last belief that is doing the justifying, and not the occurrence of the experience.[20] This would certainly conflict with the position of the theorist who holds the justification claim of two paragraphs back: for a subject can *have* experiences without having the *concept* of experience, and this theorist is likely to want to hold that such a subject's experiences still justify his beliefs. It is sometimes asked, in a question expecting the answer 'no', whether a perceptual belief would be justified if the subject believed he did not have the perceptual experience.[21] But if this is to be an objection, we would have to be considering a case in which someone has an experience of a certain subjective character, and believes he does not have such an experience. It is a question whether this is really possible. It would not be possible on any theory which in one way or another makes it constitutive of possession of concepts of the subjective character of experience that if the subject has an experience of a certain character and raises in thought the question of whether he does, then he is disposed to judge that he does.

An understandable desire to avoid certain sorts of epistemic intermediaries between our beliefs and their objects may be one source of objection to the claim that experience can justify belief. But experiences of the sort mentioned in the claim as we formulated it already carry the subject all the way to the world, at least in that the experience is characterized as an experience of the object x, a real, external physical thing, as thus-and-so. Perhaps the objection then is rather that we cannot know infallibly that the representational content of the experience really does obtain: 'if they [sensations or observations] deliver information, they may be lying'.[22] How, then, can experiences justify, given that they may be lying? We need not take this as a general sceptical question: it can be taken as a question which asks for a theory of knowledge in which the occurrence of an experience has a special role to play in ratifying certain beliefs as knowledge, and in which it is explained why it has the special role. This question I address in the last two chapters of this essay.

---

[20] There is a hint of this point in *EC* p. 476, and a more explicit statement in *ACT* p. 428.

[21] Cp. *ACT* p. 428.

[22] *ACT* p. 429.

8

Thought and Language

Throughout the above, we have freely used the notions of judgement and its content: but we have said next to nothing about the relation of these notions to language. Can we give a good account of what it is to have attitudes to thoughts without making any use of linguistic notions? In this question, thoughts are taken, as always, to be the contents of propositional attitudes: so our question is whether there is something in the nature of attitudes to thoughts in general which requires mention of language – not necessarily a language of the subject who has the attitudes – for its philosophical elucidation. I suspect that there is a gulf in this area between the view of many psychologists, who would be inclined to deny that any such mention of language is needed, and the view of some philosophers.

Our question is one about conceptual elucidation rather than one about modality. It will not suffice to answer our question affirmatively to show that there can be languageless beings with genuine attitudes to thoughts. It is indeed highly implausible that all attitudes with content require possession of a language: the spatial reasoning and thought of one of Koehler's apes tells against any such requirement.[1] But there is

[1] As Wittgenstein noted: cp. his *Remarks on the Philosophy of Psychology*, (Blackwell: Oxford, 1980), Vol. 2, Sections 186–8 and 224–9; though cp. also section 230. For Koehler's apes, see his *The Mentality of Apes* (New York: Liveright, 1976 repr.). For other examples, see Lynn A. Cooper and Roger N. Shepard, 'Turning Something Over in the Mind', *Scientific American,* **251** (no. 6), December 1984, pp. 114–20.

no contradiction in holding simultaneously that a philosophical explanation of one concept must make use of another and that nevertheless something can fall under the first without falling under the second. No one doubts that what it is for an object to be a piece of currency must be explained by means of the concept of an exchange of goods or services between two parties; but there is no difficulty in the idea of a piece of currency which is never actually exchanged. Perhaps 'possible object of exchange' is in some respect analogous to 'content of a possible object of linguistic expression'.

I shall be answering our question affirmatively, siding with some of the psychologists and arguing that no general mention has to be made of linguistic notions in an account of attitudes to thoughts. It will be convenient to label the position to be defended here that of "the theorist of thought". The earlier chapters may be taken as sketching a positive theory available to the theorist of thought of what is involved in having propositional attitudes to particular contents, and more particularly what is involved in judging them. We will suppose the theorist of thought to have adopted some account roughly along those lines. His task is now one of answering challenges to the effect that certain components of that account cannot be elucidated without mentioning the ability to use or to understand language. More particularly, this challenge may be made on three fronts. First, a challenge may be made from the agreed point that thoughts are structured entities; a second challenge may be based on the requirement of the expressibility of thoughts in language; and a third may be made from a consideration of the relations between the attitude of judgement and the practice of assertion. Again, I shall merely be locating and outlining a possible position; there will surely be many rejoinders and further rounds of the argument than are given here. I am most concerned to outline the *kind* of argument available to a theorist of thought.

The battle on the first front starts from the agreed point that thoughts are essentially structured. A critic may wonder whether a theorist of thought can give any explanation of this fact without abandoning what is essential to his position. Certainly the theorist of thought cannot consistently regard this structure as conceptually derivative from the structure of sentences which can be used to express the thought.

But this critic fails to realize that the theorist of thought already has what he needs for a good answer in his substantive theory of content. An adequate account of thoughts according to which they are individuated by reference to canonical acceptance conditions will already entail that thoughts are essentially structured. I argued in Chapter 4 that for a thought to have a certain constituent is for that thought's canonical acceptance conditions to possess a more or less complex feature. Anyone whose judgements manifest that pattern of canonical acceptance conditions is *ipso facto* judging a structured thought. The thought's structure and constituents are intrinsic to it on this account in the sense that it is impossible for someone to be judging that very content, and not to be judging something with the given structure and constituents. In a completed theory, one would actually display the canonical acceptance conditions for the whole content as a resultant of the contributions to canonical acceptance conditions made by the constituent modes of presentation.[2] It may be that in some cases the relevant feature of the pattern of canonical acceptance conditions in virtue of which a thought has a given constituent cannot be present without the ability to give some expression to the thought in language, or to understand a linguistic expression of it. This is not plausible for primitive observational contents about a thinker's environment; the question is open for more sophisticated contents. But there does not seem to be an entirely general argument here, applicable in every case in which there is structured content, to the philosophically

---

[2] One might attempt this for simple cases using the indirect specifications of canonical evidence employed in *Sense and Content*. But I would now regard that as unnecessary, an artifact of trying always to force statements of canonical acceptance conditions into 'that . . .' clauses which are supposed to stand in some form of equivalence relation to the content. If we follow the model of Chapter 2, sharply separating mental states and contents as components of canonical links, a derivation of the canonical evidence for a complex from specifications of the contributions of its constituents will be a more complex and less familiar thing; and the outward-looking method complicates matters further. But it would say directly what gives the complex in question the structure and constituents it has.

derivative character of the structure of thoughts from the structure of linguistic expressions.

The theorist of thought must also give an account of the expression of thought in language. It must be an account according to which the very same thoughts and attitudes of which he gives an essentially non-linguistic theory may still be expressed in language; and it must also explain the distinctive relations between such expression and understanding a language. The theorist of thought can discharge this obligation if he says the following.

When a sentence s has the sense that p on someone's lips, the following is true of him: the conditions whose obtaining would give him reason to judge that p are precisely those which give him reason to think that an utterance of s would in fact be true. ('Conditions' here must include not only contents which give reasons for belief but also the occurrence of experiences and other mental states.) This identity of conditions holds in actual circumstances, and in any counterfactual circumstances in which s retains for him the sense that p. When such an identity holds, let us say that the subject meets condition (I). The theorist of thought can use condition (I) in his account of expression. The whole topic of expression is extremely difficult: a good theory has, amongst other things, to characterize the relation between the expression of states with content and the expression of such states as happiness, dismay or anger. We will confine our attention here to indicative sentences which do not contain an embedding of a sentence within some synonym of 'I believe that' or 'I ___ that' for some other propositional attitude verb ___. The suggestions here must of course eventually be displayed as a consequence of a general theory which covers all sentences – but let us walk before we run. The theorist of thought can use (I) by saying that someone's utterance of a sentence s is an expression of his belief that p iff: s is intentionally produced (under its structural description), in part for the reason that he thinks that s is true, and he meets (I). Since intentionality, and the occupation by truth of a certain place in one's intentions, are required by this definition, structured states which are systematically caused by the contents of a thinker's attitudes are not necessarily states by which the thinkers *express* their beliefs. We can think of beings who, quite beyond their control, have foreheads which display visibly structured states that are correlated with the contents of their judgements. These visible states are not, intuitively, expressions of belief, nor are they declared to be so by this account. The account needs refining, but it is plausible that the components which do explanatory work in what follows would remain after the refinement.

It is a virtue of this account that it suggests a sharp explanation of the difference between describing one's beliefs and expressing them. In expressing them, one is aiming at truth about the world. According to the definition of expression, the sentence is uttered because it is thought true, and the conditions which would give reason to judge it true are the same as those which would give reason to judge that p, for some p. But when a thinker describes his thoughts, he aims at the truth of a description of his mental states and events.

An account incorporating (I) can explain the fact, emphasized by Dummett in his critique of the "map-reference view" of language, that there is no room for the possibility that two sentences, both of which are understood, determine the same *thought* – not just the same truth value – in two different ways.[3] In understanding the utterance, as Dummett says, we grasp the thought itself, the thought which is its sense. Any theory which denies this is defective. But the theorist of thought will not only not deny it: he can offer a positive explanation of why it is so. We will number his premises:

(1)   If the two sentences s and s' determine the same thought in different ways, then there will be some circumstances in which, while they retain their actual sense, it is reasonable to judge one of them true while not judging the other true.

This is just an elaboration of what is implicit in the two sentences' determining the same thought in different ways. But in our discussion a few paragraphs back we argued that

(2)   In any circumstances in which a sentence means that p on someone's lips, the conditions which would lead him to

---

[3]*The Interpretation of Frege's Philosophy, op. cit.*, p. 41ff., and especially pp. 43–4.

judge that the sentence is true are the same as those which would lead him to judge that p.

It follows from (1) and (2) that

(3)   The conditions which would lead the thinker to judge the thought which is the sense of s are not the same as the conditions which would lead him to judge the thought which is the sense of s'.

Now it is part of the conception of the thoughts we are talking about that

(4)   If there are conditions which will lead someone reasonably to judge one thought but not to judge a second, then the first and second thoughts are distinct.

(4) just follows from the individuation of Fregean thoughts by considerations of informativeness. From (4) and (3) it follows that

(5)   If s and s' determine the same thought in different ways, then the thoughts which are the senses of s and s' are distinct.

The consequent of (5) is incompatible with its antecedent, and so the antecedent of (5) is false: two sentences never determine the same thought in different ways. Since it has been argued from premises which are necessary, we can conclude that it is not possible that two sentences determine the same thought in different ways. That is what the theorist of thought had to show. All of the premises are available to the theorist of thought. It is also worth noting that this argument does not rely on any particular substantive theory of content, not even on the general view that content is determined by certain acceptance conditions.

The point can be argued equally either on the side of perceptual reception of an uttered sentence, or on the side of production. Someone who utters a sentence, and thereby expresses a belief that p, is such that the reasons he would have for judging that his uttered sentence (perhaps thought of in a distinctively action-based way) is true are identical with those he would have for judging the thought which it expresses. *This* can be so even in such extreme examples as those found in some cases of brain damage, where a speaker is a competent producer and user of a language, saying things as appropriate as your or my utterances, and yet cannot understand that language when it is spoken to him.

Even if we grant the theorist of thought everything which he has built up so far – the account of the identity of thoughts, why they are structured, the account of expression – his critic may still say that the notion which has been used in harness with that of a thought, *viz.* judgement itself, cannot be explained without reference to language. As Dummett puts it, 'judgement, rather, is the interiorization of the external act of assertion'.[4]

Dummett's reason for viewing judgement and assertion as related this way round

> is that a conventional act can be described, without circularity, as the expression of a mental state or act only if there exist non-conventional ways of expressing it; for instance, we can describe the convention governing a gesture of greeting by saying that it is used as an expression of pleasure at seeing somebody, only because it is possible to express such pleasure without the use of the conventional gesture.[5]

The principle here stated as a necessary condition of regarding something as a conventional expression of a mental state or act is surely at least a sufficient condition for so regarding it: for when that condition is met, what makes the conventional act an expression of the mental state or event is in part its association with or replacement of the non-conventional mode of expression. But is the condition necessary? That is, is it necessary for regarding an utterance of a sentence as a conventional expression of a mental state that it be possible to express that state non-conventionally?

For the sake of argument, let us accept the principle that there cannot be a non-conventional, nonlinguistic expression of belief and judgement, in the way there are non-conventional expressions of pleasure. We can label this principle "the modal datum". While one conceivable explanation of the modal

---

[4] *Frege: Philosophy of Language*, First Edition *op. cit.*, p. 362.
[5] *Ibid.*

datum is that belief and judgement have to be philosophically elucidated by reference to their possible expressions, there is another explanation. This is that there is something special about the expression of states with content which explains the datum. The modal datum itself is neutral on which explanation is correct. The point is another illustration of the distinction between modality and priority. From the fact that necessarily all F's are G's – all expressions of belief are in a language-like system – nothing follows about the relative priority of F and G: for someone who holds that the concept of an F is in some way prior to that of a G may offer some other explanation of the modal truth consistently with his theory. Earlier we agreed, on behalf of the opponent of the theorist of thought, that the possibility of something being F without being G is not sufficient to establish that the concept of something's being F is philosophically conceptually prior to that of something's being G: now we are arguing, for a different instance, that it is not necessary either.

The alternative explanation of the modal datum the theorist of thought offers will be this. Since thoughts are essentially structured, anything which allows for the expression of particular thoughts and reflects their structure must itself be a structured system; it will have the syntactic features of a possible language. On the account of the expression of belief outlined earlier, what is produced in an expression of belief must be intentionally produced under the structural description of it which correlates with the structure of the thought it expresses. In general, rational agents will act intentionally in that way only if there is some hope that others will appreciate the correlation of what they intentionally produce with a judgeable content. They may be wrong about whether others will know of this correlation; but that they act in this hope is enough to justify the description of the expression as conventional, in the sense that matters here. So the theorist of thought concludes that, because of the special features of thoughts and of expression, there cannot be an expression of belief which is not in some language-like, conventional system – which was the modal datum.

On the positive side, opponents of the theorist of thought such as Dummett have said that assertion as a practice is to be understood in terms of the conventions governing the use of those sentences which are understood as having assertoric force.[6] The theorist of thought need not and should not deny that. For part of, or a consequence of, those conventions is that a speaker is to use a given indicative sentence s to transmit a certain piece of information that p; a rational speaker will do this by uttering s only if he believes that p – if he does not believe that p, he will not take himself to be transmitting information by uttering the sentence. An honest speaker successfully conforming to the conventions will perforce apply the same standards in assessing the question of whether p as he does in assessing whether s is true; and so we can equally say, given (I) and the account of expression, that a practice of assertion is a practice of conventional use of sentences for belief expression. These are just two points of view on the same convention.

The theorist of thought must also offer a positive, non-linguistic account of the nature of judgement and belief. Here he can appeal to the role of judgement and belief in propositional attitude psychology. Strictly speaking, we have individuated content by reference to judgement rather than belief. The reason for this is that the notion of a belief is the notion of *stored* information or misinformation. What gives a belief its content has to do, in a complex way which I have tried to capture by canonical acceptance conditions, with the circumstances under which it comes to be stored or to be removed in the presence of new information. Judgement is what precedes and is crucial to such storage: though of course more than just judgement is needed for storage (there must be transfer from short term to long term memory). Judgement has some distinctive properties – it can interrupt attention to other things, it is sometimes true to say that it is done in language – but its role of being a reason-governed attitude crucial to the storage of information is what matters for the individuation of content. Anything which has this role in other organisms would be the one upon whose properties the individuation of content supervenes.

---

[6] *Frege: Philosophy of Language*, p. 311.

So far we have been concerned to outline a positive account which a theorist of thought might present, and to say how he might meet some objections. Yet surely, it may be said, we have not shown that there is anything wrong in his opponent's view? Perhaps both directions of elucidation are possible, from thought to language and *vice versa*, and we have here two families of coordinate concepts. But in fact the critic of the theorist of thought has a weakness in his position which prevents the situation from being symmetrical. The critic will say that the beliefs and other attitudes to thoughts which we attribute to languageless creatures are bestowed analogically or parasitically; they are states which have some of the properties of the belief states of language-using creatures. But if the outline sketched thus far of the theorist of thought's position is acceptable, then this claim of analogy or parasitism seems suspect. In fact, the whole idea that the attitudes of a languageless creature must be ratified as such indirectly, via their relations to the states of a creature who does have language is made to appear like an unnecessary fifth wheel. For the theorist of thought will say that the belief states of the languageless creature may bear exactly the same relations to the states mentioned in the canonical acceptance conditions of their contents as those of the creature which does have a language. This is not a matter of analogy, but of the languageless creature being in exactly the same state as his neighbour who is endowed with language.

Can an objector insist that languageless creatures have only *subdoxastic* states, and not genuine beliefs? A sign of a subdoxastic state is that it is not inferentially integrated with other content-possessing states, and consequentially it does not have the full array of possible manifestations of a genuine belief.[7] But the candidates for belief amongst a non-linguistic creature's states certainly need not have these marks: the belief that he can reach the ceiling with a stick can and does play a role in combination with many different beliefs and desires of a

---

[7] See, for instance, G. Evans, 'Semantic Theory and Tacit Knowledge', Section III, in *Wittgenstein: To Follow A Rule*, ed. S. Holtzman and C. Leich (London: Routledge and Kegan Paul, 1981).

non-linguistic primate. Indeed we need to apply the doxastic/ subdoxastic distinction *within* the psychology of a non-linguistic creature. The subpersonal states implicated in the creature's perceptual processes may, for instance, involve operations analogous to carrying out certain computations: we will want to say that these computations involve concepts and principles which the creature does not employ at the level of its genuine beliefs, desires and intentions. For the proponent of the objection we are considering, these concepts and principles would have to be at a third, sub-subdoxastic level: but there seems no good reason here for insisting on three levels rather than the original two.

These considerations in favour of the theorist of thought suggest, incidentally, an incompatibility in the views of those who want to hold both that the theorist of thought is mistaken in his general view of the relations between language and thought, and also that sentences' having the content they do is a matter of their "cohering" in the right way with the extralinguistic context and with other sentences. For if there are mental states and events which cohere in the same way with the extralinguistic context, and with other states, the question arises of why they cannot be regarded as directly having the same content as those sentences.[8]

Nothing in the theorist of thought's position licenses fanciful attributions of beliefs to languageless creatures. Constraints of the types I was aiming to describe in *Sense and Content* must be fulfilled if such attributions are to be correct, in particular the constraints on the attribution of spatial concepts and, for any family of concepts attributed, the Tightness Constraint. Certainly in some cases there may be sound arguments showing that a particular concept could not be grasped without the possession of a language; and in intermediate cases, it may be that, as a matter of contingent fact, possession of a language, allows the grasp of a much wider range of concepts than would otherwise be possible.[9] But neither of these

---

[8] One writer of whom this question could be asked, and whose phraseology I have used in its formulation, is Wilfrid Sellars: cp. especially 'Behaviorism, Language and Meaning', *Pacific Philosophical Quarterly* **61** (1980), pp. 3–25, esp. pp. 9, 10 and 14.

[9] A particularly striking example of this was found by the Premacks: it is a case in

possibilities shows that, as a consequence of the general nature of judgement and content themselves, thought cannot be explained without reference to language.

which some language-trained apes succeed in non-linguistic match-to-sample tasks on which apes with no linguistic training fail. See, for instance, David Premack and Ann James Premack, *The Mind of an Ape* (New York: Norton, 1983), pp. 39–41.

PART IV

KNOWLEDGE AND CONTENT

9

Knowledge

Nozick's well-known theory is a starting point for any contemporary discussion of knowledge.[1] The core of his theory is this: someone knows something iff (1) it is true, (2) he believes it, (3) if it weren't true, he would not believe it and finally (4) if it were true, he would believe it. That last condition is to accommodate the case of someone who is in a tank on Alpha-Centauri, being stimulated to believe that he is in such a tank: he could fulfil the first three conditions, but, Nozick says, he would fail on the fourth.[2] The reason Nozick gives is that in nearby possible circumstances in which he is still in the tank, but stimulated to believe something else, he would not believe that he is in such a tank. Nozick's account is later refined by addition of a relativization to methods of coming to believe things. He writes:

> Let us define a technical locution, S knows, via method (or way of believing) M, that p:

---

[1] *Philosophical Explanations* (Cambridge, Mass.: Harvard University Press, 1981). Page references in the text are to this volume.

[2] On both Stalnaker's and Lewis's semantics, a counterfactual 'If p were the case, then q would be the case' is true if p and q are both true. See, respectively, Stalnaker's 'A Theory of Conditionals' reprinted in *Causation and Conditionals*, ed. E. Sosa (Oxford: O.U.P., 1973), and Lewis's *Counterfactuals* (Oxford: Blackwell, 1973): both works contain a defence of this feature. So if either of these semantics gives the right class of valid counterfactual formulae, Nozick's condition (4) read literally is redundant – it is implied by his first two conditions. I shall be taking it that Nozick's true intentions are given by the immediate use he makes of condition (4).

(1) p is true

(2) S believes, via method or way of coming to believe M, that p

(3) If p weren't true and S were to use M to arrive at a belief whether (or not) p, then S wouldn't believe, via M, that p

(4) If p were true and S were to use M to arrive at a belief whether (or not) p, then S would believe, via M, that p (p. 179).

This notion of knowing via a method is then used in the final account of knowing *tout court*:

S knows that p iff there is a method M such that (a) he knows that p via M, his belief via M that p satisfies conditions (1)–(4), and (b) all other methods via which he believes that p which do not satisfy (1)–(4) are outweighed by M (p. 182).

In fact Nozick's theory counts some inferential beliefs as knowledge which are not in fact knowledge, and fails to count some as knowledge which are so. One of the cases Nozick discusses can be used to introduce this cluster of issues. He considers a person who comes to believe that there is a vase in a certain box. This person in fact sees an illuminated hologram of a vase, and the box itself alternates between showing an illuminated hologram and a real vase. The case, as Nozick notes, can be set up in such a way that it is only because there is a real vase somewhere in the box that an illuminated hologram of a vase is sometimes displayed. There will be versions of this case on which, by Nozick's definition, the subject is counted as knowing that there is a vase in the box. For if there were no vase, he would not have a visual experience as of a vase (caused by the hologram) and would not believe that there is a vase in the box; and we can set up the example so that in nearby circumstances in which there is a vase, there is also an illuminated hologram of it in the box, and so he does believe there is a vase in the box. Nozick remarks that his verdict that this is knowledge is somewhat counterintuitive, but adds

however, we certainly do not want to hold that a person knows that p only if he has no false beliefs about the process via which he comes to believe that p. The Greeks had many false beliefs about the visual process (p. 190).

I would say that this person does not know there is a vase in the box, and that his belief is not knowledge because it rests on a false belief: the demonstrative belief that *that* (perceptually presented) vase is in the box. When he is seeing a hologram, the demonstrative fails to refer; or if the thought is put in the form "*that* is a vase and it is in the box", then the first conjunct is false. The case is, then, to be assimilated to others which are not knowledge because the belief rests essentially upon some other false belief. Harman's compelling "no false lemmas" requirement is violated.[3] Nozick is right in saying that false beliefs about the perceptual process need not prevent the acquisition of perceptual knowledge. But those false beliefs of the Greeks about the perceptual process were not *operative* in producing such perceptual beliefs as 'that is a shield' or 'there is a vase in that box'. In the hologram case, however, the existential belief that there is a vase in the box rests essentially on the perceptual demonstrative belief; were that belief abandoned, then the subject would as things are have no reason to believe that there is a vase in the box.

As one would suspect, this case can be generalized to present a difficulty in explaining Gettier cases for anyone who uses Nozick's conditions.[4] In one classical Gettier case, the subject infers from suitable evidence to the false intermediate conclusion that Smith owns a Ford, and moves from that to the true final conclusion that someone he knows owns a Ford, a conclusion he does not know to be true. As has occasionally been noted (and as is noted by Nozick himself), in such a Gettier case it could be that if none of the subject's friends had owned a Ford, then he would not have come to the conclusion that Smith owns a Ford: perhaps Smith hired a Ford because some of the subject's friends own Fords. This modification – a Gettier case with the counterfactual twist – does not incline us to say that the case is then one of knowledge. We have here the same structure as in the example of the vase: Nozick's conditions for knowledge can be fulfilled with respect to the final conclusion consistently with that conclusion resting essentially on beliefs which are false.

[3] G. Harman, 'Inference to the Best Explanation', *Philosophical Review* **74** (1965), pp. 88–95.
[4] E. Gettier, 'Is Justified True Belief Knowledge?' *Analysis* **23** (1963), pp. 121–123.

Nozick feels no tension in allowing that there are Gettier cases with the counterfactual twist because, he tentatively suggests, his own discussion of methods incorporates the Harmanian requirement of no false lemmas. Nozick writes:

> Perhaps our account can yield [that requirement], by treating "infers it from q" as the method the person uses to arrive at his belief that p (p. 189)

The way he intends this assimilation to work is apparently this: when q is false, someone using this method, which we are to hold fixed (p. 189), would still believe that p by inferring it from q, even if p were also false. But this is too strong as a way of capturing the case: it would rule out ever obtaining knowledge by deduction from known premises by known principles of inference. The method which Nozick is holding fixed is this: inferring p from q. The subject can still be applying this method even when p is false: the deductive method can be the same whether or not its premises are true. Nozick seems in effect to be appealing to the condition (3') which he takes as a consequence of his (3):

(3') (not-p and S infers p from q) $\Box\!\!\rightarrow$ not-(S believes p).

But no subject can ever meet (3'), since it is *a priori* false: given that inference here is a matter of reaching beliefs, no one can infer p from q without believing p.

The way Nozick hopes to incorporate Harman's requirement also undermines the natural treatment of perceptual beliefs in Nozick's own account. In those cases, your method is, for instance, that of judging whether it's raining on the basis of your having an experience, or not, as of its raining. If that is the method then Nozick ought equally to be prepared to argue that your perceptual belief that it is raining is not knowledge, on the ground that if that method ("judging on the basis of the occurrence of an experience as of its raining") were applied even when it is not raining, then you would believe that it is raining when it is not. That would exclude all cases of perceptual knowledge. Suppose on the other hand one insists that the truth of the counterfactual 'If it were not raining, the subject would not have any experience as of its raining' *is* relevant: then the question arises of why the corresponding counterfactual 'If it were not the case that p, then he would not believe that q and so there would be no question of his inferring anything from q' is not relevant in the Gettier cases with the counterfactual twist.[5] A parallel critical argument could be mounted for the case in which knowledge is acquired from the knowing testimony of others: we do not want to be forced to say that such knowledge is never acquired on the ground that if someone were to apply the method (hearing someone suitable assert that p) even when it is not the case that p then he would believe something false. Perhaps Nozick would reply that we are to hold the method constant in a genuinely inferential case, but not in the case of noninferential knowledge acquired by perception or testimony. But then this puzzling asymmetry would need a rationale. If we are to avoid such problems, we need a better treatment of inferential knowledge.

Suppose I believe that this piece of chalk (visually presented to me) was imported from France. I may believe this because (i) I have been told by an official that all chalk supplied in Oxford University is imported from France (ii) I believe this is a piece of chalk supplied by this university and (iii) I believe this university is Oxford University. Here we can speak of the *total method* I use on this occasion in reaching my belief that this piece of chalk was imported from France. The total method is an ordered, tree-like structure which is illustrated in the diagram on the next page. In this diagram, each node corresponds both to a method and to a belief reached using that method on this occasion. The method used in reaching the belief about all the chalk supplied in Oxford is that employed in the acquisition of a belief by testimony, that of taking a suitable person's utterance at face value; the method used in reaching the belief that this particular piece of chalk is supplied by this university is a result of taking one's visual experience at face value; and so on. The beliefs which result from the operation of these methods are then input to an inference drawn by applying

---

[5] The situation is especially puzzling, because Nozick, who holds that knowledge is not closed under known logical implication from known premises, allows that deduction from known premises by principles known to be valid does yield knowledge if the subject would not believe the premises, were the conclusion to be false (p. 321). But this last condition is *met* in the Gettier cases with the counterfactual twist.

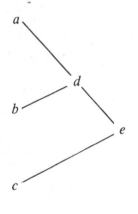

a: taking experience at face value
("This is Oxford University")

b: taking experience at face value
("This chalk is supplied in this
university")

c: trusting the utterance of a suitable
official ("All the chalk supplied in
Oxford University is from France")

d: identity elimination ("This chalk is
supplied in Oxford University")

e: universal instantiation ("This chalk
is from France").

universal instantiation. So the methods corresponding to
nodes *a, b, c* and *d* can be said to be prior to, or earlier than, the
use of universal instantiation at node *e* in the total method. The
total method employed in a particular case is given by
combining the various submethods in the right tree-like
fashion. It will be important for later purposes to note that the
initial segments of a total method will then themselves also be
methods: thus the subtree whose nodes are *a, b* and *d* is a
method of reaching a belief, on this occasion the belief that this
piece of chalk is supplied in Oxford University. It will also be
convenient to introduce one last piece of terminology. For a
given method and a given content that *p*, we can distinguish
those conditions which when fulfilled and when one is using
that method lead one to believe that *p* from those which lead
one in the same circumstances to believe that ~*p*. We will call
the former *positive input conditions* (for *p*, for that method) and
the latter *negative input conditions* similarly.

Actually we need to be more careful here. Later we shall
repeatedly ask questions such as 'Would this method have led
to a true belief if the subject had been in such-and-such a
situation?' But consider someone who takes his ordinary

experiences at face value, and comes to believe 'This room is sunny'. There is a clear and for many purposes important sense in which if he were in a second, different, room, and there formed a belief 'This room is sunny', he would be forming a different belief: it would be about a different room. Yet we will want to be allowed to say that if the second room looks sunny but in fact is not – he is on a film set – the very same method he used in connection with the first belief leads in the second room to a false belief. The same point applies to other indexical constituents of a content: even in the case of a first person constituent, we want to be able to raise the question of whether a method for forming first person beliefs is reliable for another person. It seems that when the content is indexical, the method is a method for forming what we called in Chapter 8 a belief in a certain *type* of indexical content.[6] A method may be a method for reaching a certain type of content, which together with the thinker's context at a given time fixes a unique truth-evaluable content. Often in what follows I will slip into making general statements about "a method for reaching a given content that *p*": this should always be read "a method for reaching a given content that *p* or a given type of demonstrative content".

Now suppose we could find some property P such that it is required for knowledge that every initial segment (proper or improper) of the total method by which a belief is acquired have that property P. In our case of the belief that this chalk is from France, such an account would demand not only that the total method, corresponding to the whole tree, have the property P; it would require also that the subtree whose nodes are *a, b* and *d* have that property P, and that nodes *a, b* and *c* severally possess it too. Such an account will have the following virtue. Let us call *fully unified* any theory which supplies one single condition which both inferential and noninferential beliefs may satisfy, and in virtue of which, according to the theory, they are knowledge. Now consider any account which mentions some property P and says that for knowledge it is required that every initial segment of the total method by which a belief is acquired have that property P. Such an

[6] For the case of belief, this is what Perry captures in his terminology of the belief *state*: cp. his paper 'The Problem of the Essential Indexical', *Nous* 13 (1979), pp. 3–21.

account can be part of a fully unified theory, since in the noninferential case, the method which is employed (*e.g.*, taking one's experience at face value) could still have that property *P*: the case would be special simply in that the method has no proper submethods. A noninferential belief could still strictly satisfy the universally quantified condition that all the proper or improper submethods of the method by which it is reached have the property *P*.

For the moment, as a condition to be refined below, I suggest that we take *P* to be this property of a method *M*: use of *M* in the actual world and in nearby possible worlds yields a belief true in the world in which the method is used. Inserting this into our suggestion, we obtain this condition (U):

(U)   A belief is knowledge only if it is reached by a total method such that use of any of its proper or improper initial submethods yields in the actual and in nearby possible worlds a belief true in the world in which it is used.

This needs some explanation.

To say that there is a nearby possible world in which *p* is true is just to say that it could easily have been that *p*. There is no obvious threat of circularity here, because this 'could' is not epistemic in any straightforward way. It can be true that for all we believe, something might easily have come about, even though it could not really have come about easily at all; and conversely. Nor does this notion of nearness seem to be one that can be explained only in terms of knowledge. It seems rather to be one we draw upon even when epistemological distinctions are not in question, as when we discuss the different degrees of safety to which a nuclear power plant may be built. There we are considering how easily we are prepared to allow circumstances to come about in which there is a leak. This notion of nearness needs further philosophical elucidation: what matters here is that there is such an intuitive notion on which we can draw.

Any theory, like Nozick's or the present theory, which uses a notion of nearness, has the resources for explaining how empirical knowledge can consistently have two properties. First, the methods by which it is reached are in principle almost always fallible; and second, there is nonetheless a relatively strong sense in which if something is known, the knower cannot be mistaken. By 'a relatively strong sense' is meant a sense stronger than is given simply by the necessitation of the conditional 'if something is known, it is true'. As McDowell has argued, there are forceful intuitive objections to theories that do not allow a stronger sense than mere necessitation of the conditional.[7] We are, for instance, uneasy with the suggestion that there can be two situations in which a subject has the same reasons for believing a given content, and in which the *only* reason for saying that in the one case he knows it and the other he does not is that the content is in fact true in the one and false in the other. Any theory using nearness can explain the first property of empirical knowledge by noting that for almost any method, there are some possible worlds in which it does not yield true beliefs: of course, on the present theory, these will not be nearby worlds. The second property is explained because according to theories employing nearness, the method used *does* yield true belief in all nearby worlds. Take any modal operator O such that it is sufficient for Op that in all nearby worlds, p is true. Then we can assert outright this conditional with O in its *consequent*: 'if someone knows that p, then O (he is not mistaken using his actual method)'. The two properties of empirical knowledge are consistent because the class of possible worlds relevant to explaining the fallibility of methods is the class of all possible worlds under consideration, while the class of worlds relevant to the explanation of the second property is the different, less extensive class of nearby worlds.

The condition (U) is of a form which allows it to be part of a fully unified account. Since it is only a necessary condition of knowledge, whether a theory is fully unified will depend on the nature of the other conditions; but (U) itself will be an essential step towards full unification. (U) also implies Harman's requirement that there be no false lemmas in the chain of reasoning by which a belief is reached. For if one of the intermediate beliefs is false, consider the submethod of the

[7] See his 'Criteria, Defeasibility and Knowledge', *Proceedings of the British Academy* **68** (1982), pp. 455–79, esp. pp. 458–61.

total method by which that intermediate belief was reached. Clearly the positive input conditions for that intermediate belief relative to that submethod were fulfilled; but since the belief is false, use of that submethod does not yield true belief in the actual and nearby possible worlds. Hence that submethod fails to have the property which every submethod has to have if the final belief is to be knowledge. So we obtain Harman's requirement that the final belief is not knowledge if there is an intermediate false belief in the reasoning. Equally, if any of the intermediate beliefs, even if true, is not knowledge because the submethod by which it is reached does not have the property required of it by (U), then any final belief based on it is not knowledge either.[8] We will give an example illustrating this later.

There is unclarity in (U) over the intended characterization of the method used on a particular occasion. Our beliefs that this is grass, that a building, might be said to be reached *via* the method of taking one's experiences at face value. But we can imagine a thinker who, with an enthusiasm for the exotic, also takes his experiences as of unicorns and ghosts at face value. If the method is individuated as widely as 'taking experience at face value', it does not lead to true belief in nearby worlds. But this should not prevent you or me from knowing that this is grass, that a building; and it should not so prevent our enthusiast either, if his impulsive, uncritical enthusiasm is confined to a suitably limited subject-matter.

This example suggests that the relevant boundaries of a method should be tied much more closely to the particular transitions made on the occasion when the belief was acquired. That experiences as of unicorns lead to false belief is irrelevant to the status of beliefs caused by his seeing the lawn. But too much detail in the characterization of the method leads to the opposite problem. Take the familiar case of the subject in an area where, unbeknownst to him, mere barn-facades, as well as real barns, are to be found. An experience of a brown barn will be an experience of it as having a certain particular shade of

---

[8] This derivation of Harman's requirement makes no specific reference to epistemic communities; so it undermines the claim that only by citing properties of communities of potential knowers can the requirement be explained. For that claim, see R. Shope, *The Analysis of Knowing* (Princeton: Princeton University Press, 1983), at p. 216ff.

brown. Suppose all barn facades never have that particular shade, for technical reasons not easily altered. Then an experience as of a barn of that shade will not, in nearby circumstances, lead to a false belief of the form 'this is a barn'. Nevertheless a belief caused by such an experience will not, in those circumstances, be knowledge; and intuitively this is because the method is, in those circumstances, defective. We need to find an intermediate level for characterizing the method.

I suggest that the boundaries of the method relevant to the status of a belief as knowledge should be determined by the thinker's operative reason for forming the belief. The particular shade of brown played no part in our last subject's reason for believing that that was a barn in front of him. What was operative was that the experience was *as of a barn*; and taking experiences of that wider type at face value will lead to false belief, when the subject is in front of one of the barn-facades. On the other hand, the unreliability of experiences of unicorns is outside the scope of our other subject's reason for believing it is grass beneath him, *viz.* that it looks like grass. Henceforth we will take methods as individuated at this intermediate level.

But suppose the shade of brown in question in the preceding paragraph is B, and that our subject comes to believe "That's a B barn". Then it *will* be true that the occurrence of an experience as of a barn of shade B was operative in the subject's reason for forming the belief; here our tactic of appealing to the subject's operative reason will not help, yet intuitively this is not a case of knowledge.[9] However in this example we can discern a structure in the subject's reasons. He has a reason for believing "That's a barn"; and, given it is, he has reasons for believing it's a B barn.[10] Now the method employed in the first part of this structure is that of taking an experience of a barn at face value: and in the case in which there are mere barn-facades around, use of this method will in nearby circumstances lead to

[9] Martin Davies raised the question: as this essay goes to press, I heard Saul Kripke make essentially the same point in his 1985 Gareth Evans Memorial Lecture. Many of the morals Kripke draws from his striking examples dovetail well with the conclusions reached in this chapter.

[10] I put it this way rather than as a structure of reasons for believing a conjunction since it is not quite clear that all colour predications split up conjunctively.

false belief. So his belief 'That's a barn' is not knowledge. But we already argued above that it is a consequence of (U) that if any of the intermediate beliefs on which a final belief rests is not knowledge, then the final belief itself is not knowledge; hence in this example 'That's a B barn' is not knowledge either. This is the promised example in which failure of a true belief to be knowledge prevents a belief resting partly upon it from being knowledge.

Theorists who have said that for a belief to be knowledge it must not be an accident that the belief is true may be tempted to say that their theory implies Harman's requirement of no false lemmas. On a naive no-accident theory, this does not seem to be so. The sense in which in a Gettier case with the counterfactual twist the subject has a true belief by a lucky accident is manifestly not that if the belief were not true, the subject might still have it – for in these cases he would not. Perhaps then his belief is accidentally true at least in some more general sense? It may be said that the point is rather that the subject, in inferring that one of his friends owns a Ford, is employing a quite general total method his willingness to apply which is in no way restricted to the special circumstances of the counterfactual twist, and will lead him to false beliefs in other cases. But this is not right either. Suppose a person were protected by undetected, beneficent supervisors who so manage things that in any nearby world in which the subject applies the same total method as he does in one of these cases with the counterfactual twist, it leads to a true final belief. However beneficent and ingenious these supervisors, if they hope thereby to ensure that their charge will always gain knowledge, they are under an illusion. This is not a problem which can be solved by high technology or sufficient funds: for if the intermediate beliefs on which their charge's final conclusion essentially rests are false, that final conclusion is still not knowledge.[11]

---

[11] These points cast doubt on Dretske's claim that his 1981 theory is not troubled by Gettier cases. In 'Précis of *Knowledge and the Flow of Information*', *Behavioral and Brain Sciences* **6** (1983), pp. 55–63 at p. 95. Dretske writes: 'The problem is evaded in the information-theoretic model, because . . . one cannot get into an appropriate informational relationship to something false'. The final beliefs in the cases with the

Is this example of the supervisors excluded as a case of knowledge on a no-accident theory because it is surprising that the subject's belief is true in cases with the counterfactual twist? Surprise is an epistemic notion, whereas the idea of a no-accident account seems to have to do with the mechanisms there are in the world, whether their presence is surprising or not. We would also have to ask, 'Surprising given what information?'. If we are given the information that the subject has seen one of his friends, Smith, driving around regularly in a Ford, then it is not surprising that his belief that one of his friends owns a Ford is true. If we are given too that Smith does *not* own a Ford (and perhaps that the subject has no other reason for it) then it may well be surprising that the belief that one of his friends owns a Ford is true. If we are given yet more information, about the activity of the supervisors, then again it is not surprising that the belief is true. For the suggestion about surprise to work, we must be given the information that an intermediate belief *en route* to the subject's final conclusion is false, and not a lot more. If we are given that, Harman's requirement would then be a consequence: but it would be a consequence of the particular information we allow in assessing what is surprising. We would not have justified writing in just that kind of information on the basis of the naive no-accident requirement.

This is not to denigrate the conception underlying the no-accident requirement as an essential ingredient in an account of knowledge. On the contrary, our (U) itself is an instance of that conception. But it does apply the conception to each submethod of the total method by which a belief is reached: the examples given suggest that the conception cannot be applied neat to the output of the total method, without regard to the properties of the beliefs formed *en route* to the conclusion.

If several total methods meet the condition on their submethods formulated in (U), then so too will the larger total method which consists of those methods together with a

---

counterfactual twist are true, and by Dretske's definition there would be an informational relationship in the most recent example in the text. The intermediate beliefs are indeed false, but to appeal to this is to invoke a requirement of no false lemmas which has not been established by the information-theoretic approach.

deductive principle applied to their output at the final stage. This ensures that if a set of beliefs in the premises of a valid deductive principle meet the necessary conditions for knowledge so far formulated, so does a belief in its conclusion inferred in accordance with that principle.

The status of abduction – taken here to include any inference purportedly to the best explanation – as a possible source of knowledge is more complex.[12] Besides its intrinsic interest, the status of abduction matters here because we will be placing some weight upon it in Chapter 10. Nothing ensures that abduction yields truths, either in the actual world or in nearby worlds; an abductive inference can be of the correct form to explain phenomena known to occur, can be careful, imaginative and better than its current rivals, but yet still lead to a false conclusion. Even if it does yield a true belief, that belief will not necessarily be knowledge. So how does abduction ever yield knowledge? Perhaps we should distinguish two requirements for a belief acquired by abduction to be knowledge. First, an explanatory suggestion is proposed which would explain certain phenomena; and second, the hypothesis is accepted as true on the basis of further experiment, evidence or reasoning. The method consists not just of thinking up a simple hypothesis to explain the data: it also comprises a policy of not accepting the hypothesis as true unless one has a sufficient range of evidence which, in the circumstances, ensures that if the hypothesis were not true, one would not believe it. (The evidence does not, presumably, have to do that with respect to all conceivable circumstances – it could not.) Thus for instance it is by now the case that if DNA were not to have the shape of a double helix, we would not believe it to do so. Until this counterfactual became true, the hypothesis about its shape was not knowledge.

There are some remaining observations on (U) before we move on. One is that (U) does not solve all the uniformity problems which arise. So far we have been considering only necessary conditions for knowledge. When we consider sufficient conditions for noninferential knowledge, these

---

[12] At this point, I have profited from a discussion of an earlier draft with Paul Horwich.

sufficient conditions must either have analogues in the case of inferential knowledge, or else we must explain why it does not matter that they do not. Second, there are familiar examples in which it is not even true that there is a method by which the subject reaches his belief – not even in the broad sense in which a method is employed in reaching perceptual knowledge. These cases we will consider in the next chapter. Third, (U) accommodates knowledge of logical truths which are, say, known by a proof in a sequent calculus in which all assumptions are discharged. As a method of reaching beliefs, provision of such a proof certainly yields beliefs true in the actual world and in nearby worlds in which it is used.

(U) takes it that, when there is a method by which a belief is reached at a given time, the belief is knowledge only if this condition is met:

(R) Use of the method in the actual and in nearby worlds at that time yields a belief true in the world in which it is used.

The fact that a method meets (R) will, in the case of empirical knowledge, be grounded in part in the existence of mechanisms: mechanisms which can be physical, physiological, psycho-logical, sociological, economic, or any combination of these. When someone comes by looking to have knowledge which he expresses by saying "That's a house", these mechanisms would include those which sustain the proper functioning of the eye, and those social and biological mechanisms by which the kinds of perceptible objects around us continue to be those which match the three-dimensional representational content of our experiences. Intuition also immediately suggests that (R) needs further strengthening, because we ought to require that the subject's employment of the method he actually uses be suitably related to its *being* a method which fulfils (R). A method, however reliable, selected by spinning a roulette wheel does not meet this further condition. Perhaps we should add in parallel with conditions already accepted that in nearby worlds, the subject also uses the given method to determine the truth of the content in question. It would be at this point that such a requirement could ratify the importance of evolutionary epistemology. For the mechanisms outlined by evolutionary epistemologists, those of blind variation and selective retention, of generation and selection routines, are precisely processes which can lead to an organism's employing, in the actual and in nearby circumstances, methods which on the whole meet (R).[13]

We should always require more for knowledge than production of true beliefs on a particular occasion on which a method is applied, even when it is applied by a mechanism which, as things actually are, is sensitive to the truth of those beliefs. Consider the case of a businessman who arrives from abroad at an airport in a dictatorship. He picks up the first newspaper on which his glance alights, and believes what he reads in it. Suppose there is a government apparatus of censors and news revisors, who regularly rewrite journalists' copy. These news managers are, though, short staffed and can only work at some of the papers. They choose which papers to visit at the start of each day. It so happens that the paper picked by our businessman was not censored, and was written by wholly honest, reliable reporters. We can suppose too that the news comes in after the news managers have selected the paper they are to visit. In these circumstances it can be true that if the businessman's paper says something, then it is true; if it weren't true, it would not say it; and if there were other important news, it would have truly reported it. Nevertheless, we have an intuition that the businessman does not gain knowledge from reading this paper (even though his beliefs may in some important sense be a result of the truth of their content). For there is nothing in his method and the surrounding circumstances which ensures that he is reading an unrevised paper: the newsagent could easily have placed a different paper in the slot for which he reached, and our businessman would then have read a managed newspaper. Our earlier discussion requires us to determine the method used from the thinker's actual reason for forming his beliefs, and in this example his reason is just that he read the content in a newspaper purchased in that country; in nearby worlds, this method does not yield true beliefs. This remains so even if by coincidence it happened that

[13] For a fine survey and discussion of evolutionary epistemology, see D.T. Campbell, 'Evolutionary Epistemology' in *The Philosophy of Karl Popper*, ed. P. Schilpp (La Salle, Ill.: Open Court, 1974), Vol. 1.

every particular occasion on which someone did employ such a method happened to be one on which he read an uncensored newspaper.[14] The example shows that a nearness requirement always demands more than just the existence of certain mechanisms in the actual world.

Reflection on such examples points up a difference between the concept of knowledge and the concept of perception of an object or event. The region of someone's brain responsible for the production of visual experiences may sometimes receive input from his sense organs, and sometimes from another region, in which case hallucinations result. Its being connected with the sense organs may be as unreliable as our businessman's reaching for an uncensored newspaper. But when the brain is connected to the sense organs, the subject may be perceiving objects and events: yet the businessman does not know what he reads in the uncensored newspaper he picks up. Perception of a physical object seems more closely connected with relations of causal explanation in the actual world, and knowledge more closely tied to counterfactuals.[15] So, leaving aside arguments over the treatment of a subject's reasons in his account, we ought to be attracted to the counterfactual form of Nozick's theory.

There are five *prima facie* reasons why we should accept (U) and its consequence (R) as necessary conditions for a noninferential belief to be knowledge. The first, of course, is that they can be integrated into a fully unified account of inferential and noninferential knowledge.

The second reason concerns knowledge obtained by luck. The issue here is raised by Nozick's condition (4), which reads

---

[14] It does not seem right to say that the reason this case is not one of knowledge is that had there been a small departure from the actual course of events – one of David Lewis's "small miracles" – then the subject would have had a false belief. (See Lewis's 'Counterfactual Dependence and Time's Arrow' *Nous* 13 (1979), pp. 455–76.) For that is also true in undisputed cases of knowledge: it may take only a small departure from the actual course of events to fail to notice an occurrence of "not" in a sentence. The question is not whether the departure from the actual course of events is small, but whether it could easily have come about.

[15] It is much more plausible, though, that the propositional idiom '*a* perceives that *p*' entails '*a* knows that *p*.'

If p were true and S were to use M to arrive at a belief whether (or not) p, then S would believe, via M, that p.

Nozick says that he means this conditional in a sense in which it is not sufficient for its truth that the material conditional with the same antecedent and consequent be true. He says that what he requires, if formulated in possible worlds terms, is that in worlds in which the antecedent is true and which are close to the actual world, the consequent is true. Nozick says (p. 177) that this fourth condition rules out as knowledge the belief you have when floating in the tank on Alpha-Centauri that you are in such a tank, on the ground that in nearby worlds in which the scientists give you different experiences and beliefs, you do not believe you are in the tank.

Yet it is obvious that a subject can gain knowledge fortuitously.[16] He may happen to be looking the right way at the right time: there may be no relevant notion of closeness on which it is not a nearby world in which at that time he looks the other way. To this it may be tempting to reply that Nozick's condition should simply be reformulated: it ought to require only that in nearby worlds in which the positive input conditions relative to the subject's actual method for the given belief are fulfilled and that the content of that belief is true, he has that belief. Nearby worlds in which the positive input conditions are not fulfilled would not then be counterexamples to this condition. However, this proposed condition cannot exclude any examples, because it is a logical truth. The positive input conditions for a method relative to a given content are just those which, when a subject is applying that method, lead him to believe that content: it is necessarily and *a priori* true that in any world, nearby or not, in which a subject is applying a given method and the positive input conditions for that method are fulfilled, then he believes the content. It seems clear that Nozick does intend us to take his fourth counterfactual to be one which has in its antecedent that the subject is applying the given actual method M in the nearby world: his full fourth condition read 'If p were true and S were to use M to arrive at a belief whether (or not) p, then S would believe, via M, that p'.

[16] See G. Forbes, 'On an Attempted Refutation of Scepticism', *Philosophical Quarterly* **34** (1983), pp. 43–52.

Though we know in advance that a logical truth will not exclude any examples, it will be helpful to see in more detail how unwanted examples are let through by this unsatisfactory revision. Let us take a subject who still has his body, but whose afferent and efferent nerves linking brain and body have, unknown to him, just been severed: his brain is linked instead to a computer. This subject may judge 'My body is cold', on the basis of an experience as of his body's being cold caused in him by the computer. His body may in fact be cold. This subject does not know his body is cold: but after these latest revisions we cannot account for that fact in the way Nozick hoped. We cannot now relevantly argue 'The subject does not know his body is cold because the scientists using the computer in a nearby possible world could have fed him different experiences which would lead him to believe something false': for in those nearby worlds, the positive input conditions for the belief, relative to the given method, *viz.* the occurrence of an experience as of his body being cold, are not fulfilled. Note that Nozick's condition (3), that if the belief were not true, the subject would not believe it, could still be met by the case, so that we cannot blame it for the lack of knowledge. The computer may have default settings of the experiences to be caused in the subject: one such, perhaps randomly selected in the past, may be an experience as of his body being cold. If the computer warms up, non-default settings chosen by the scientists will be implemented; the non-default possibilities never include that of the subject's feeling cold. The computer will warm up if the subject's body is not cold, since it is adjacent to his body. In these circumstances, it will be true that if the subject's body were not cold, he would not believe it to be cold. So we have now a case which is not knowledge, although all the conditions in the account currently offered to Nozick are fulfilled. On the account I will develop later, the subject in the example of the preceding paragraph does not have knowledge because his experience as of his body being cold is not a *perception* of his body being cold.

This may make one wonder whether we ever need some revised version of Nozick's (4), and if so, how it is to be formulated. Even in Nozick's original case, of the vat subject who believes he is in a vat on Alpha Centauri, the question arises. Suppose a normal human goes to bed on earth one evening. That night, the Alpha-Centaurian scientists extract his brain. They immediately take it to Alpha Centauri and connect it to the hallucination-producing computer. There they feed to it experiences as of waking up normally on earth, as of meeting scientists who want to take him to Alpha Centauri and put his brain in a vat. Our subject has a hallucination as of travelling there, and of being placed on the operating table. These experiences could give him reason to believe he has become a brain in a vat on Alpha Centauri. But again, the apparent perceptual-demonstrative beliefs on which this belief that he is in a vat on Alpha Centauri rests ('That planet receding into the distance is Earth', 'This is a Centaurian operating theatre') are untrue: they fail of reference. No belief resting on them will be knowledge. So could we not account for the absence of knowledge without invoking the fourth condition?

But in fact not all examples in which someone on Alpha-Centauri believes he is so need be like the one just elaborated, and Nozick is right that it is initially intuitive to require something along the lines of his fourth condition. A formulation close to the spirit of Nozick's fourth condition and which is not a logical truth would be this: in nearby worlds in which it is the case that p, and the subject applies his actual method M *and it yields a verdict on whether or not p*, then the subject believes that p. (R) is to be read similarly. (It is, though, a question needing further investigation whether the work Nozick intends to be done by his fourth condition would in fact all be covered by a good formulation of the other conditions being proposed here.)

A third reason for accepting (R) is that it implies a suitably qualified form of the condition for knowledge that p which requires that were $\sim p$ to be true, the subject would not believe that p. This is essentially Nozick's (3), and its core is highly intuitive: how can someone know something if, using the same method, he might easily believe that p even when it is false that p? Nevertheless, it needs to be restricted. I know I am in London. I know that the principle of alternation-introduction is valid. I infer that either I am in London or I am not a brain in a vat on Alpha Centauri. I know this last alternation, if I know whatever I infer from known premises by alternation-introduction, which I also know to be valid. Even Nozick (not wholly consistently) remarks that it 'surely carries things too far' (p. 230) to deny that knowledge is closed under this logical implication. But it need not be true that if that alternation were not true, I would not believe it. The negation of the alternation is logically equivalent to the conjunction that I am not in London and am a brain in a vat on Alpha Centauri: and we can elaborate an example in which in the worlds closest to the actual world in which I am in a vat on Alpha Centauri, I do believe the alternation. So Nozick's condition (3), presumably meant to apply to any possible example, is too strong.

We should add the restriction that it is only of nearby worlds that we require that if p is false there, the subject does not believe it there: so the restricted version of (3) states that in any nearby world in which p is false and the subject uses his actual method M to determine whether or not p, he does not believe that p. Worlds in which the alternation of the preceding paragraph is false are not nearby (if our ordinary beliefs are right) and so are not counterexamples to the restricted principle. The restriction is wholly in the spirit of the ideas underlying Nozick's theory of tracking, which I have been endorsing. In the case of positive tracking – believing something when it is true and one has the evidence – Nozick restricted the requirement to nearby worlds: there is at least no obvious reason to demand more than this in the case of negative tracking too.

(R) implies condition (3) so restricted. We can argue by contraposition. Suppose that the restricted (3) is false. Then there is a nearby world w in which p is false and in which, using his actual method M the subject does believe that p. But the belief that p is false in w: so use of the method M does not in each nearby possible world yield a belief true in that world.

A competing proposal would be that we should react to the alternation inference about Alpha-Centauri not by restricting Nozick's (3) to nearby worlds, but by restricting it to noninferential knowledge. Two considerations make this untempting. First, the condition (4) about positive tracking of noninferential beliefs still needs restriction to nearby worlds. No one would say that if a perceptual belief 'This is flat' is to be knowledge, it must be that in *every* possible circumstance in which the belief is true and the subject applies his actual method, he has the belief. (The possible circumstances will include those in which the light is misleading, his perceptual system is defective, and so forth.) So in restricting (3) to nearby circumstances, we use a notion which this competing proposal will have to draw upon anyway. Second, the argument that (R) entails (3) restricted to nearby worlds was not confined to noninferential knowledge. Part of the attraction of (R) was that it applies to inferential knowledge too. So if the considerations in favour of (R) carry any weight, the weight should be taken to support (3), restricted to nearby worlds, for inferential knowledge too.

Condition (3), and the related issue of the closure of knowledge under known deductive principles, have as a result of Nozick's theory become connected with the question of radical scepticism. Nozick holds that we can know many of the things we ordinarily take ourselves to know – that this is a desk, this is flat, that I am in London – but we do not, says Nozick, know that the radical sceptic's possibilities do not obtain. These beliefs fail (3), for were, say, you to be in a vat on Alpha-Centauri being stimulated in a way which causes you to believe you are not there, you would still believe that the sceptic's possibility does not obtain. The present chapter is no place for an extended discussion of the major topic of radical scepticism. But the asymmetry we have found between positive and negative tracking in Nozick's account bears on his treatment of scepticism. For when the asymmetry is corrected in the way we suggested, the position Nozick seeks to occupy vanishes. It was not counted as an objection to your knowing 'This is flat' by looking, that in some circumstances the light will be behaving very oddly: because those are circumstances which, as things actually are, could not easily have been realized. Similarly, if the world is as we believe it to be, it should not be taken as an objection to your knowing that you are not in the tank on Alpha-Centauri, that were you there you would still believe you were not: for your being there is not a circumstance that could easily have been realized. If the tracking requirements are restricted to "nearby" possible circumstances, we can know the sceptic's possibilities do not obtain (and we would not need to deny closure to block their threat); if the tracking requirements are not so restricted, we will know almost nothing, not even 'This is a desk'. For one who, like Nozick, asserts that we do not know that the sceptic's possibilities do not obtain, it is more difficult than Nozick suggests to confine the effects of radical scepticism to belief about sceptical possibilities. In the account I have been developing, nothing has so far emerged to undermine the view that a belief obtained by a known deductive principle from beliefs which are knowledge is itself knowledge: in fact, we saw that (U) encourages the view. The sceptic is more, not less, challenging in the direction I am proceeding.

This was a detour from our discussion of (R). The other two reasons for accepting (R) concern its explanatory power. Reason number four is supplied by the ability of (R) to explain the following principle (T), whose truth has been noted by many writers,[17] and which we can call *The Transmission Principle*:

(T) If x knows that p and tells y that p and y understands x's utterance and comes thereby to believe that p, then y comes to know that p.

Any good account of knowledge must explain why the Transmission Principle is true in the cases in which it is. It is not enough to speak metaphorically of conveying knowledge or acquiring it or passing it on. These images are good because a Transmission Principle is true, and what we need to know is why it is true. The most satisfying form of explanation here consists in a derivation of the principle from independently motivated conditions for knowledge. If we accept (T) without giving such a derivation, we will not have shown knowledge to be a unified, non-disjunctive concept.

Such a derivation should also explain why the principle has to be qualified – for it certainly does need qualification. Suppose Mary sometimes comes to believe that it is raining by looking, and sometimes by deduction from astrological principles. On occasions of the former sort, she knows it is

---

[17] For an early statement, see E. Sosa, 'The Analysis of "Knowledge that P"', *Analysis* 25 (1964–5), pp. 1–8, at p. 8.

raining; on occasions of the latter sort, she does not. But if on an occasion of the first sort, she tells her friend that it is raining, he does not come to know that it is raining. Intuitively for him to have knowledge, we require not just that Mary know that it's raining, but that he in coming to believe it from Mary's say-so be employing a method which yields true belief in nearby circumstances: and his method does not do so if Mary sometimes engages in astrological reasoning. Similar points apply to the persistence of an informant's honesty, and indeed to the whole class of persons from whom the subject is prepared to acquire beliefs about a given subject matter. These qualifications involve no commitment to the idea that knowledge acquired by testimony is based on an actual inductive inference about the reliability of informants. The qualifications are required by the clear deliverances of intuition about examples, rather than by some prior theory of knowledge acquired by testimony.

The most we can hope to achieve in the way of a derivation of the Transmission Principle at this stage is to show that if (R) is true, and x satisfies the antecedent of (T), then y meets the necessary condition (R) for knowledge. We cannot go further until we have sufficient conditions.

So suppose x knows that p, and that the method M he uses yields true belief in the actual world and in nearby possible worlds. We have also added that x uses M in nearby possible worlds to determine whether p, and that in nearby worlds, he is still trustworthy; and that the same goes for others in the collection of people from whom y might acquire the belief that p. Now consider y's method of coming to believe that p in the circumstances with which the Transmission Principle is concerned, *viz*, finding it asserted by someone in this collection of people: we take it that the operative reason for the formation of the belief is of that kind. It follows from the conditions we have supposed that in the actual world, and in nearby possible worlds, y's method yields true belief. This is what we needed to show.[18]

---

[18] The case could also be argued separately for the restricted version of Nozick's (3) we endorsed. Assume the antecedent of (T). In nearby worlds in which $\sim p$, x does not believe that p. In nearby worlds in which x does not believe that p, y does not believe that p. Hence in nearby worlds in which $\sim p$, y does not believe that p.

A final reason for accepting (R) is that it can explain some of Harman's examples about evidence the believer does not possess.[19] One of Harman's examples is of someone in a foreign country who reads in the first edition of a newspaper that the dictator has been assassinated. The later editions, which the subject does not see, deny the reports of an assassination: these later editions are produced on the instructions of those who in fact assassinated the dictator. Nozick notes that his condition (4) explains why the reader of the first edition does not have knowledge: in the nearby worlds in which he encounters the later editions, he does not believe in the assassination. One ought to expect quite generally from (R) itself that in many cases in which there is evidence contrary to a subject's belief, that belief is not knowledge. If the subject might easily have encountered that evidence, then he would, applying his actual method of reaching his belief, come to believe something false: so (R) would not be fulfilled. (This was also true of the businessman who purchased the newspaper.) A reflective subject who accepts the present account of knowledge and believes he knows that p will realize that he cannot consistently admit the existence of such evidence unpossessed by him: this is one way he can be committed to believing that there is no such undermining evidence.

In this chapter I have modified Nozick's account of knowledge and in particular given a more significant role to inferential structure than it received in his original formulation. While this may have had some interest in itself, my main purpose has been to provide a plausible framework of conditions for knowledge on which we can draw in the next chapter: there I will argue that an account of knowledge is incomplete unless it invokes distinctions

---

[19] G. Harman *Thought* (Princeton, N.J.: Princeton University Press, 1973), p. 143; and 'Reasoning and Evidence One Does Not Possess', *Midwest Studies in Philosophy* V (1980), pp. 163–182. I should say immediately that (R) by no means explains all Harman's examples. One would certainly need to say something different about those cases in which there is evidence not possessed by the believer and which is evidence not that his belief is false, but that his evidence is incomplete. These issues are too delicate for a brief treatment.

drawn from a substantive theory of content. In this last chapter, the epistemological strands we have been tracing out here and the earlier strands concerned with content will merge.

10

Rationality Requirements, Knowledge, and Content

What are the links between epistemology and an acceptance-condition theory of content? Why have I included material on knowledge at all in an essay on content? In this chapter, I will begin to fill in some of the hitherto missing links. We earlier outlined substantive theories for some contents in terms of grounds and consequences, for others we used a three-tier model, and for a notion like negation the model was different again. But at a very general level, we can say that these are all theories of content which appeal to canonical acceptance conditions. A canonical acceptance condition for a content is a normative condition about acceptance of the content which has to be mentioned in an account of what it is to grasp the content. Using this general notion, we can then formulate a link between knowledge and the theory of content. I will be arguing that the conditions for a belief to be knowledge I have outlined so far are necessary but not sufficient; I will argue that we need to add to them the requirement that the belief be rationally held, in a sense to be explained; and I will argue that what makes a subject's holding of a belief rational is in part a matter of his relations to the canonical acceptance conditions of the content of the belief. In effect I will be making a set of claims which are at one end of a series of possible views, ordered by increasing adoption of features of the position I will be defending. One can conceive of a theorist who holds that there are indeed rationality requirements for knowledge, but that these requirements have nothing particularly to do with the content of the belief; or again of a theorist who holds that such requirements do have to do with content, but that content is not to be individuated by canonical acceptance conditions. My position is like that of this last theorist, but goes further in that I do take content to be determined by canonical acceptance conditions.

Not every noninferential belief meeting (U) of the preceding section is knowledge. So far we have made no requirement that the method by which a belief is reached has to be appropriate to its content if that belief is to be knowledge. There is such a requirement. A noninferential belief 'That liquid (perceptually presented) is water' may be knowledge, when based on the experiences of looking and tasting. But the same method by itself is not sufficient to make the belief 'That liquid (perceptually presented) is H_2O' knowledge: when the method does not involve inference or memory, looking and seeing would be quite irrational as a method of reaching the belief that that liquid is H_2O. If we can conceive of someone reaching the belief by that method, the belief would not be knowledge. We can elaborate the example by adding that in nearby possible worlds, only H_2O has that distinctively neutral taste; with this elaboration, we can obtain an example in which, for this irrational method, Nozick's conditions (3) and (4) are met, and so are the conditions we endorsed in the preceding section. But this would still not make the belief that that liquid is H_2O into a piece of knowledge.

The existence of a rationality requirement can also be illustrated by considering a case of Sosa's, as reported by Nozick:

> As an effect of brain damage, a person is led (irrationally) to believe he has brain damage, which he would not believe if he didn't have brain damage. However, condition 4 is not satisfied: if the brain damage had been slightly different, though using the same route to belief he would not believe he had it (p. 190).

Suppose that the subject's brain is so structured that in all the nearby worlds, brain damage leads to the belief that he has brain damage. Compare a nuclear reactor: it may be that in all the nearby worlds in which it is damaged the damage is to parts other than the core, since that is so strongly protected. (Well, it may not be, but we can conceive it.) Again, this modification of the brain damage case does not make the subject's belief any more rational, and it does not seem that it would make it knowledge. It would remain irrational when the subject believes that his brain is damaged because of distortion in his visual field, if in addition he has no reason to think that it is his brain, rather than his eye or optic nerve which is malfunctioning. Yet in either version of the case it seems that all Nozick's conditions for knowledge could be met.

In both the example of H_2O and that of the brain damage, we find ourselves wanting to say that if he is to gain knowledge, the thinker's method must be *appropriate* to the content of his belief. An exercise of a perceptual recognitional ability by itself is not enough to justify a belief about the microstructure of a substance, nor is some malfunctioning enough to justify a belief that one component rather than another of one's perceptual processing devices is damaged. In this sense, as accounts which stress the need for justification have always insisted, there is a requirement of *rationality* for knowledge: externalist conditions alone are not enough. It is a joint task of epistemology and the theory of content to explain the nature of this relation of appropriateness of method to content.

Can we account for these examples in a less general way? A competing explanation of the absence of knowledge in these cases would be this: a noninferential judgement based on a contemporary sensory experience is knowledge only if the content of the judgement is contained in the way the experience represents the world as being ("the containment condition"). The beliefs in the H_2O and the brain cases do indeed fail to meet this containment condition: the experiences on which they are based are not experiences which, respectively, represent it as being H_2O that is in front of the subject, or represent one's brain as damaged. If it were accepted, the containment condition would have to be shown to be the consequence of a general account of knowledge. But there are examples which suggest that the failure of internal rationality is a better explanation than the containment condition.

There are examples in which the containment condition *is* fulfilled, yet the belief is not knowledge: given the content of the belief, internal rationality requires more than reliance on an experience which represents that content as obtaining. Examples of this type show that the failure of internal rationality is a more general explanation of the cases than is failure to meet the containment condition, which will not cover all the cases.

Consider someone who is capable of having experiences as of one event causing another. This is not something *recherché*: anyone who sees the child's hand as knocking over the tower of blocks, or a fork-lift truck as lifting a crate, has such experiences. These experiences would not be adequately characterized as seeing an event of one type following an event of a second type. Rather, taking the experience at face value, one would be disposed to judge that the child's movement caused the tower to fall over or to judge that the rising of the fork-lift truck's arms caused the crate to go up. Such cases also display the characteristic feature of the content of experience as opposed to the content of judgement that they need not alter when additional information results in a judgement of a content incompatible with that of the experience. Even if one knows that the crate is in fact moved up by a powerful electromagnet, it may still look as if the truck is lifting it: it is precisely because the causal concept of lifting has to be used in specifying the content of the experience that it is appropriate to talk of an illusion here. It is perhaps worth adding that the acknowledgement of such experiences is quite consistent with acceptance of a regularity theory of causation: that there are such *experiences* leaves it open that causation *in the world* consists ultimately in regularities.

Take the moving shapes on the screen in a video game. We know on a moment's reflection that one light patch colliding with another does not cause the second patch to move, even though that is the vivid content of our visual impression when watching the screen. The cause of the movement of the second bright patch lies rather in the implementation of the program in the software. Now take someone who is in an environment carefully designed so that for him, on the contrary, impressions of causation are always veridical. So if someone in this environment sees one bright patch collide with another on a screen, the first really does cause the second to move: perhaps there really are bright little fluorescent objects moving around immediately behind the screen. We might imagine superior beings designing environments for simpler creatures, or for their children. Does someone located in such an environment know, without ever having checked on the fact, that one bright patch colliding with another on his screens really does cause the latter to move – as it does in fact on his screens but not on ours? It seems that we would not say that he has knowledge here. (This does not imply that he does not have knowledge of causal relations between offscreen events: he will have been in many situations which suggest that spilling coffee and the resulting dark patch on his clothes are not independent effects of a common cause.) Despite the pronouncement of intuition that we do not have knowledge in the video example, the noninferential beliefs in causal relations based on experiences as of colliding and the rest when this subject is looking at the screen *are* beliefs whose content is contained in the representational content of his visual experiences. The containment condition is met. So that particular attempt to explain the earlier examples without appealing to appropriate justifications for the contents does not apply to this case. We could also modify the example so that Nozick-like externalist conditions are fulfilled too: perhaps the superior beings design the environment in all nearby circumstances.

If we want to explain why this is not a case of knowledge, it seems more promising to argue that the canonical acceptance conditions for the holding of a causal relation would have to do ultimately with laws, however analyzed, and in any particular case – and perhaps in general – impressions of causation are only *a posteriori* associated with the relation of causation in the world, whatever it consists in.[1] In order to know that one bright

---

[1] Is it at least true that many impressions of causation must be veridical when the subject is perceiving the world around him? No: we need only to alter the case to one in which the superior beings design an environment in which, for instance, when one billiard ball strikes another and the second apparently moves off as a result, in fact both are radio-controlled. The cause of the first ball stopping and the second one moving are in, say, the machine-language formulation of some program by which the superior beings control events in the subject's environment. There does not seem to be any conceptual difficulty in elaborating this example so that virtually all the subject's impressions of causation are non-veridical.

patch causes the other to move, the subject in the imagined environment would have to know that his impressions of causation are reliable signs of the relation itself; and in the example, this he does not know. He could come to know it if he investigated the bright patches further, but then the case would either be one of inferential belief, or of a memory belief based on prior investigation, rather than noninferential belief based on sensory experience. The impressions of causation would then also be at least in principle inessential to attaining the knowledge.

An objector might agree that the subject in this example does not know that the events on the screen are causally related, but attempt to offer a rival explanation. The rival proposal would be this: the fact that a caused b does not causally explain the occurrence of the experience of causation – what explains that is the occurrence of movements of certain types, as Michotte's experiments show.[2] A causal relation, it seems, *never* explains an impression of causation. How could it? If the relation of causation between events requires those events to fall under general types related by law, a's causing b seems to be a condition of the wrong sort to explain any singular state of affairs. The point seems to hold good whether or not we accept a regularity analysis of laws: as long as a statement of law has some implications for events other than those perceived, it seems that the existence of a law is a stronger condition than that which explains our experience.[3] Such would be the objector's proposal.

I would reply that this explanation, with whose claims I agree, does not compete with the one in terms of canonical acceptance conditions I offered. If a relation is of the wrong sort to be capable of explaining the occurrence of a particular experience, we cannot *perceive* that relation to obtain between two presented things (even if our experience represents it as holding between them): we cannot perceive it in the sense in

[2] A. Michotte, *The Perception of Causality*, tr. P. Heath (New York: Basic Books, 1963).

[3] Someone might say that, like colour properties, causal relations have primary quality grounds which can enter causal explanations; but Michotte's results show that the cause of the impression of causation is motion of certain sorts, rather than any primary quality ground of causation. They also show that these motions are not the ground of causal relations.

which perception requires causation of an impression by the condition the impression represents as obtaining. Perception of the condition as obtaining cannot then be mentioned in the canonical acceptance conditions for contents concerning that relation. But that was the explanation of the example I was offering. The importance of the formulation in terms of canonical acceptance conditions is, of course, that it allows us to unify the treatment of this case with that of the others.

To someone who holds that singular causal statements can be barely true and that we genuinely perceive – not just have experiences as of – causal relations holding, these considerations should be unconvincing. The dispute would then become one about causation, if this particular example is to be defended. But other notions beside causation could serve to make the point: any notion which can enter the conceptual representational content of an experience, but the canonical acceptance conditions for instances of which does not involve experiences of the sort on which a judgement is based, would suffice to make the point. So here is another kind of example.

We see certain facial expressions as expressions of pleasure: someone with such an expression we perceive as pleased. Some of the higher non-human primates have expressions which strike us, naively, as expressions of pleasure: where in fact these expressions, which involve the baring of teeth, are threatening signs, possibly expressions of anger. Now suppose we tampered with the nervous and genetic systems of some of these primates so that what actually strikes us as a pleased primate really is a pleased primate, and the same goes for their offspring. Suppose we place these primates in the environment of some human subjects who do not know what we have done, and are naive about expression in primates. We could, again, fill out the example so that after some years it is true that in any nearby possible circumstances only altered primates exist to be encountered. Our human subjects may then form the belief of a perceived primate that it is pleased, simply because they experience it as pleased; so the containment condition is met.

In fact in this case, unlike the video example, the belief in question will indeed be caused by the primate's being pleased. But again there is an intuition that this is not enough for knowing that the primate is pleased; in the absence of any reliance by these subjects on evidence that what seems to them to be an expression of pleasure really is such – which we can readily conceive not to be the case – their belief falls short of knowledge. Intuitively, they fail a requirement of rationality. The reason they fail it may not be quite the same as in the causal example. It is perhaps more plausible that the ability to see something as an expression of pleasure should be mentioned in the canonical acceptance conditions for contents containing the concept of pleasure than that impressions of causation should be so mentioned in the case of the concept of causation. The rationality requirement is failed in the primate example because the role of pleasure in a psychological theory of primates would also be mentioned in the canonical acceptance conditions for contents containing the concept of pleasure. We will not want to regard someone as using the concept of pleasure if he does not in his judgements at least implicitly acknowledge that the fact that a type of action has been pleasurable is a *prima facie* reason for performing it in the future. The humans we imagined have no evidence that the states expressed by the primates' faces have the right role in the psychological theory.

So far we have considered only beliefs based on reasons, in the broad sense in which not only inferred beliefs, but also beliefs based on sensory experience or the utterances of others are held for reasons. But there are beliefs which are knowledge though not held for any reasons even in this broad sense. Most people in Western societies know their date of birth without possessing any reasons or justification. Even if they happen to remember seeing documents recording that date, those memories are not operative in producing the knowledge: they would know even had they forgotten all such documents. The same applies to each person's knowledge of many historical, scientific and mathematical contents.[4]

The existence of such knowledge not based on reasons leads to a fork in our path. One option is to elaborate the limited thesis that a rationality requirement applies only to knowledge

[4] Cp. E.J. Lemmon, 'If I Know, Do I Know That I Know?', in *Epistemology: New Essays in the Theory of Knowledge* (New York: Harper and Row, 1967).

based on reasons. The other option is to state and elaborate a stronger thesis which entails the limited thesis, but adds also that even for knowledge which is not reason-based, there is an analogue of a rationality requirement.

The limited option raises questions about the unity of the concept of knowledge. If we have only reliability, and not rationality, requirements for beliefs not based on reasons, then it is unclear why a transition to an inferred or any other reason-based belief should need any more than the right kind of reliability. It seems that a unified concept should have rationality requirements in both cases or in neither. Yet if at the fork in the path we take the more extensive option of saying that the rationality requirement applies in all cases, we face a different challenge: how *can* a belief not based on reasons be subject to some analogue of a rationality requirement? We need to consider knowledge not based on reasons in more detail.

The least controversial cases of knowledge without reasons are probably those of propositional belief served up by memory. We can distinguish two accounts of what makes such beliefs knowledge. We can call them the *Pure Storage Account* and the *Model of Virtual Inference.*

The leading claim of the Pure Storage Account is that it is sufficient for a belief served up by memory to be knowledge that it was knowledge when it was originally acquired, together with the fact that it has been reliably stored in a suitably content-preserving fashion. The Pure Storage theorist may add that he, unlike others, does not obscure the distinction between *accessing* a store of information and *making inferences* about the contents of that store. It is open to this theorist, but not forced on him, to extend this account to knowledge acquired by testimony: this is the case in which the subject acquires knowledge by accessing not his own, but another's, store of information.

In allowing knowledge without reasons when the belief is acquired by accessing a store of information, the Pure Storage Account need not totally abandon the requirement of internal rationality. The cases in which knowledge without reasons is allowed are not on a par with, for instance, a case in which someone's belief that there is an animal in the vicinity is caused by a smell, a smell which is in fact a wholly reliable sign of an animal, but on which the believer has no reason to rely. The cases are different. In a case of knowledge without justification, where the belief is transmitted along a causal chain, when the belief was originally formed the one who formed it must have satisfied the justification condition and any other internalist conditions for knowledge. This applies to chains of such links. Beliefs resulting from the belief originally formed inherit its credentials as a piece of knowledge; beliefs resulting from putative stored information which does not trace back ultimately to a belief satisfying the rationality conditions for knowledge cannot themselves be knowledge. In the case of the subject who forms his belief that there is an animal in the vicinity on the basis of a smell which he has no good reason to believe is correlated with the presence of an animal, his belief is not acquired from a stored belief which traces back ultimately to something formed in conformity with the rationality conditions.

In adopting this account of memory beliefs which are known though not justified, the Pure Storage Account rejects the view that memory knowledge is counted as such because it could be inductively justified. There certainly is a fundamental difficulty in the idea that memory at its most basic level could be ratified inductively as reliable. Suppose you have an apparent memory that there is a piano in the next room. You go there and do find a piano there. Can this, in the context of this attempt to vindicate apparent memory, confirm your earlier apparent memory? At the later time, when you are in the next room, you perceive the piano and have an apparent memory that you earlier had an apparent memory that there is a piano in this room. But did you really have that apparent memory earlier? Since apparent memory is up on trial, you cannot just take that as known. Yet what you need to have confirmed is that genuine past apparent memories are confirmed by later experiences: this is what you need inductively to project to the future if you are to rely on your apparent memories. If memory could be a source of knowledge *only* via inductive reasoning, this problem seems insoluble – for all later confirmation can ever give is a set of then current perceptions together with a set of apparent memories. This tells one nothing, independently of memory, of what one apparently remembered earlier. The Pure Storage Account has none of these problems.

The Pure Storage Account does not entail that it is sufficient for knowledge that a belief be obtained by accessing a store of information elements of which were known when first stored. The mechanism required for a noninferential memory belief to be knowledge is more extensive than the mechanism required for the belief originally stored to be knowledge. The more extensive mechanism will include the workings of memory itself. It will also include the mechanisms by which the modes of presentation of indexically presented objects in the originally stored belief are realigned as time passes or the thinker alters his spatial location: today's belief 'It's noisy here now' must two days later and two miles south be realigned by an efficient thinker to 'It was noisy two miles north two days ago'. A fully unified account will then have the form: a belief is knowledge if it is, or results by suitable realignment and transmission from, a belief which originally met (U) and was reached by methods appropriate to its content.[5] If either the storage or the realignment mechanism does not work properly, or is liable to fail, a memory belief which results from the storage of what was originally knowledge may not itself be knowledge. It would also be open to a slightly less pure storage theorist to say that a belief may also fail to be knowledge even without defects in these mechanisms if later evidence against the content of the belief has appeared: the stored belief may not be counted as knowledge if, for example, it cannot be reasonably believed given the subject's current total evidence. But this, the slightly less pure storage theorist can say, does not mean that when no contrary evidence appears, the thinker who accesses a stored belief must be making an inference. So much for the outlines of the Pure Storage Account.

The rival Model of Virtual Inference says that a belief held

[5] This requires qualification in examples in which there is prior conceptual impoverishment. In such cases, the stored information may not always trace back to a prior *belief*. Some of a thinker's current beliefs about what causes what may trace back to stored sensori-motor routines which proved their success in action at a time at which the subject did not even have the concept of causation. But the success of a type of routine in a wide variety of circumstances still bears a special relation to the canonical evidence for judging a causal content: a specification of such success would be canonical evidence for the truth of a causal content.

without reasons is knowledge only if a sound, and in the circumstances knowledge-yielding, inference to the best explanation *could* be made from the evidence available to the believer to the truth of his belief. There is no circularity in using the notion of a knowledge-yielding abduction here: we said what makes an abduction knowledge-yielding in the preceding chapter. The Model also requires that the evidence from which the inference can be made is influential in the right way in causing the subject to have the belief. The Model is one of virtual rather than real inference, since it denies that the thinker who has knowledge ratified by its claims is really himself making these inferences.

The Model of Virtual Inference preserves a rationality requirement in a stronger sense than does the Pure Storage Account: for it applies an analogue of a rationality requirement to the situation of the believer at the time at which the memory is assessed – it is with respect to that situation that an abductive, knowledge-yielding inference must be possible if the belief is to be knowledge.

The advocate of this model can agree with the likely argument of the Pure Storage theorist that there is no possibility of inductive ratification of memory as a source of knowledge. Harman is surely on strong ground when he says that not every example of inference to the best explanation can be seen as straightforward inductive inference.[6] Here we may just have another case: it may be said that the best explanation available for the apparent memories given the subject's experiences is simply the truth of their content, and this applies equally to apparent memories of earlier apparent memories. I will now argue briefly that there are reasons for preferring the Model of Virtual Inference to the Pure Storage Account.

It is important to be clear on the question being asked here. The question is not whether the notion of storage of information has to be used in an account of memory: for it surely does. Our question is rather what makes certain memories *knowledge*: we are asking whether we need to appeal to more than just the notion of storage in saying when a belief delivered by memory is knowledge. This is the reason for the

---

[6] G. Harman, 'Inference to the Best Explanation', *op. cit.*, p. 90.

qualification "Pure" in the labelling of the Pure Storage Theorist. The Virtual Inference Theorist can consistently, and had better, hold a storage theory of memory: his claim would then entail that such storage is necessary but not sufficient for memory knowledge.

Consider someone who, when asked for the year in which Hume died, answers that he died in 1776. Suppose that there is not a rational, sound abduction to be made from this belief to its truth. We can suppose the subject to be someone who has had no contact with philosophy since his undergraduate days thirty years ago, and has certainly not heard of or thought about Hume since. Of his present beliefs resulting from those days, some match the content he absorbed then in lectures and reading and some do not; for the purposes of this example, we will take it that the subject is not aware of that. This description of the case so far is consistent with his belief about Hume being stored neurophysiologically in a way in which it could not easily be distorted over time. That it is so securely stored may not be something which can be inferred from his present general tendencies to be right about some areas, wrong about others.

When he is asked, it strikes this subject as being true that Hume died in 1776. But does he know it? There is an intuition that he does not, and this is what the Virtual Inference Model predicts. But it is hard for the Pure Storage Account to explain why it is not knowledge: the storage of the information may be as reliable as human memory ever is.[7] The intuition can be strengthened by supposing that the subject also has the false belief that Voltaire died in 1779, and has no more reason for believing that he is right about Hume than that he is right about Voltaire. It matters here that the question for us is whether the subject knows, rather than whether his judgement is in some broad sense a delivery of his memory mechanisms (which it surely is).[8]

[7] So it is not denied that on one notion of information storage and transmission, the subject's belief can carry the information that Hume died in 1776; it can do so without the subject knowing that Hume died then.

[8] It is plausible that remembering *that p* entails knowing that *p*. So if we say this subject does not know that Hume died in 1776, we must deny that he remembers that Hume died then. But we can still say that he has a belief whose source is the faculty of memory.

The defender of the Virtual Inference Model also need not be conflating accessing a store of information with making inferences about it: his theory is just that the former is not enough for knowledge.

How might the Pure Storage theorist try to treat the memory belief about Hume as not a case of knowledge? He might say that it is not knowledge because the belief about Hume could easily have been as insecurely stored as that about Voltaire. But this need not be true in the example. At the time he acquired the information, our subject might have been intensely interested in Hume, and beliefs on subjects of intense interest might be securely stored. He may now have entirely forgotten that he had this interest. Another attempt might be to claim that it is not knowledge simply because other beliefs are not securely stored. But this reason applies to all memory beliefs: it would exclude the possibility of someone reliable in some areas but not in others ever having memory knowledge not based on reasons. According to the Virtual Inference theorist, the possibility of a knowledge-yielding abduction from the subject's own current information distinguishes the cases. There is no such abduction to the truth of his belief about Hume. There could not be, because we have described a case in which any abduction available to him which could be given to the truth of his belief about Hume could equally be given for his belief about Voltaire: but the latter belief is not true. For his beliefs about his own name, address and occupation, on the other hand, he has a vast body of information best explained by the hypotheses that these beliefs are true.

It would also be hard to apply to testimony the treatment the Pure Storage Account accords to memory. There is a strong intuition that a belief is not knowledge if it is acquired by testimony for which there is no inductive or abductive argument available to the believer to the truth of the testimony. Can we gain knowledge from an isolated sentence inscribed in a language we understand on a slab of stone which we date to 1000 years ago and which is excavated from a site of which we know nothing historically? There would be nothing to exclude it as knowledge if we apply the Pure Storage Account's model straightforwardly to testimony. In fact the case for the Virtual Inference Model (if not something more) seems at least as strong for testimony as for memory. Memory beliefs held without justification are not reached by any method at all: the trained mnemonist is exceptional precisely in that he uses a technique. We do not need to use any technique or method in answering the question 'What is your name?' But in acquiring beliefs by testimony, we will not trust just anyone about anything; and when we unreflectively trust a colleague about the time of a meeting, we have a reason in the sense that we do so because we think it is the kind of thing he would be in a position to know and has no reason for deceiving us.[9] If all that matters is not that we think that our colleague is in a position to know and is honest, but that he is so, it would be hard to explain why we do not correspondingly gain knowledge from the thousand-year old slab.

I have argued that a rationality requirement for knowledge exists, and that it is present in some etiolated form even for knowledge not based on reasons. But I have still to deliver on the promise to connect these rationality requirements with the canonical acceptance conditions for a content. Even when a belief is held for reasons, and the content believed is one which has canonical grounds, it is not required for the belief to be knowledge that it have been reached *via* knowledge of one of its canonical grounds. In general, there is no type of content at all knowledge of which has to be reached *via* possession of reasons for thinking that what is mentioned in the canonical acceptance conditions holds good. A present-tense observational predication of a perceptually presented

---

[9] As against these considerations, it may be thought a reason for holding that no inferences, virtual or actual, are involved in ratifying beliefs resulting from testimony as knowledge that it is *a priori* impossible that most assertions are mistaken. (On these issues, see C.A.J. Coady, 'Testimony and Observation' *American Philosophical Quarterly* **10** (1973), pp. 149–55, and M.A.E. Dummett, 'Realism' *Synthese* **52** (1982), pp. 55–112, esp. p. 108.) Suppose we grant for the sake of argument that it is impossible. From the fact, even the fact known to you, that most F's are G's, it does not follow that any F you encounter and believe to be G, you also know to be G provided it is G. Otherwise, knowing you are in a country in which the President is elected by absolute majority and in which voting is compulsory, you will be counted as knowing of anyone with whom you are presented that he voted for the elected President, provided only that you believe it and it is true. Knowledge must require more, and the same applies to testimony. The whole question of the status of testimony of course needs a more detailed treatment than it will receive here.

object may be knowledgably inferred from a high-level theory; or again, a logically complex content may be knowledgably inferred by a principle of inference which would not itself be mentioned in, but would rather be derived from, a statement of canonical acceptance conditions for contents containing certain logical notions; and a thought of almost any form may be known as a result of an inference to the best explanation. There must be such a thing as coming to know a content by a means other than by the route of first having reason to believe that what is mentioned in the canonical acceptance conditions holds.[10] Correspondingly, the structure of a subject's justification for his beliefs will often diverge from the structure given by the relative position of the contents of his beliefs in the Grand Partial Ordering of contents: the two structures should not be conflated.

A better strategy is to introduce an auxiliary concept, which is linked both with canonical acceptance conditions and with knowledge. The auxiliary notion is that of a belief being, as we said earlier, *rationally held*. A noninferential belief based on reasons – such as one resulting from testimony or perception – is rationally held if the reasons are good reasons; a non-inferential belief not based on reasons is rationally held if the form of rationality requirement we outlined above in the Virtual Inference Account is met; and an inferential belief is rationally held if rationally inferred from rationally held beliefs. A belief is knowledge only if it is rationally held in this sense. The relevance of a content's canonical acceptance conditions to epistemology is that they help to determine whether, in given circumstances, a belief with that content is rationally held.

Consider, for example, a case in which a belief is held because its owner has certain experiences, and in which the belief is noninferential (except possibly for dependence on a belief that his perceptual systems are minimally functioning). Any such belief will be knowledge only if two conditions are met. The first condition is that the canonical acceptance conditions for the content believed mention perceptual

---

[10] This sentence adverts, using the present framework, to the phenomenon with whose characterization Dummett grappled in 'The Justification of Deduction', *op. cit.*

experience of a type which includes the experience which is the subject's reason for forming the belief. This first condition may fail either because the canonical acceptance condition for the content in question does not mention perceptual experience – as in the causal examples – or because the reason-giving experience is of the wrong type. In each type of failure, to obtain knowledge of the content from such experiences the subject would have to infer it from some further substantive known belief which more or less directly connects such experiences with the content in question. A second condition for the original belief to be knowledge, when the experience is of the right type, is that the canonical commitments of the content of the belief must be rationally incurred: as we saw, these commitments may be to the truth of a family of other contents (as with universal quantification), or they may be to the occurrence of certain kinds of perceptual experience, or to a combination thereof. If this second requirement, that the commitments be rationally incurred, is not met, the belief would not be rationally held. The requirement would not be met by someone who takes his experiences at face value, even though he knows he might well be looking through an Ames window. A belief that a presented object is cubic based on a perception of only one of its faces and no auxiliary information would be deficient on this requirement too.

The underlying principle here is that good evidence for accepting a content must support, directly or indirectly, the claim that the truth conditions determined by the canonical acceptance conditions do really hold. Thus in the case of knowledge obtained by abduction of a content determined by its canonical commitments, the abduction must give a thinker good reason to believe that all the canonical commitments of the hypothesis which is abduced do really obtain.

In the case of a belief not based on reasons, the role of canonical acceptance conditions is less direct, but still present. There is a distinction to be drawn here which is correlated with the distinction between the cases in which a belief is based on reasons and that in which it is not. In the former cases, the believer's reasons are reasons for judging that content itself. In the latter cases, consider the factors mentioned in the Virtual Inference Account to which a subject must be sensitive if a belief is to be knowledge when it is not formed for reasons. These are factors from which a rational, knowledge-yielding abductive inference is possible to the effect that the source is on this occasion yielding a true content, rather than being factors which directly support the content itself; the content itself is supported only indirectly, by being delivered as true by a source ratified as reliable. In this second type of case canonical acceptance conditions are present only at a distance: but it remains the case that a full account of rational confirmation of the source's yielding true contents will involve the possession of reasons for believing the truth conditions determined by the canonical acceptance conditions of those contents are fulfilled. In this case, as in the others, if we do not mention canonical acceptance conditions, we will be unable to say what is distinctive of knowledge.

Index